Homemade Baby Food Pure & Simple

Your Complete Guide to Preparing

Easy, Nutritious, and Delicious Meals

for Your Baby and Toddler

Connie Linardakis

PRIMA PUBLISHING
3000 Lava Ridge Court
Roseville, California 95661
(800) 632-8676
www.primalifestyles.com

Published by Prima Publishing, Roseville, California. Member of the Crown Publishing Group, a division of Random House, Inc.

PRIMA PUBLISHING and colophon are trademarks of Random House, Inc., registered with the United States Patent and Trademark Office.

Warning—Disclaimer
This book is not intended to provide medical advice and is sold with the understanding that the publisher and the author are not liable for the mis-conception or misuse of information provided. The author and Prima Publishing shall have neither liability nor responsibility to any person or entity with respect to any loss, damage, or injury caused or alleged to be caused directly or indirectly by the information contained in this book or the use of any products mentioned. Readers should not use any of the prod-ucts discussed in this book without the advice of a medical professional.

Library of Congress Cataloging-in-Publication Data
Linardakis, Constantina.
    Homemade baby food pure & simple : your complete guide to
    preparing easy, nutritious, and delicious meals for your baby and
    toddler / Connie Linardakis.
        p.   cm.
    Includes index.
    ISBN 0-7615-2790-7
    1. Cookery (Baby foods). 2. Infants—Nutrition. I. Title.
TX740.L56   2000
641.5'622—dc21   00-058891

01 02 03 04 DD 10 9 8 7 6 5 4 3
Printed in the United States of America

First Edition

Visit us online at www.primapublishing.com

To my mother, Angelina Nepolis, my official chef of good,
natural food and an unbelievable source of courage.
Thanks for your gifts of unconditional love
and absolute trust that supplied my self-esteem,
thrill of discovery, and joy in life.

To my son, Michaelis, for blessing me with
his arrival and being my baby gourmet!

CONTENTS

ADVISORY PANEL OF CHILDREN'S NUTRITIONAL EXPERTS

The following people made invaluable and professional contributions to this book:

Gayle Povis Alleman, **M.S.**, **R.D.**, author of *Save Your Child From the Fat Epidemic* (Prima) and a registered dietitian with a master of science degree in nutrition from Bastyr University.

Nikos Linardakis, **M.S.**, **M.D.**, author of fourteen medical books for McGraw-Hill, New York.

Stephanie Mori-Nakao, **R.N.**, **B.S.N.**, **C.L.E.**, general staff nurse in obstetrics and gynecology, home visiting nurse, and certified lactation educator for St. Mark's Hospital Salt Lake City, Utah.

Alexander Golbin, **M.D.**, **Ph.D.**, director of the National Institute for Sleep Disorders in Chicago and former chairman of child psychiatry at Cook County Hospital in Chicago.

Rachel Jones, **M.S.**, vice-president of media relations for the Dairy Council of Utah with a B.S. in nutrition from the University of Utah in Public Health and Nutrition and a M.P.H. from the University of California at Berkeley.

ACKNOWLEDGMENTS

Homemade Baby Food Pure & Simple is a special book that could not have been completed without the support and encouragement of my family, friends, and medical experts.

A very special thank you, first and foremost, to my husband, Dr. Nikos, for his many talents and for encouraging me to finish this book. Not only is he an acclaimed medical book author with McGraw-Hill Publishers, but his ability to keep adding "positives" to life make it enchanting to be his partner.

Special thanks to Stephanie Mori-Nakao, R.N., B.S.N., C.L.E. (certified lactation educator) for her professional evaluation of information on breastfeeding and bottlefeeding. Ms. Mori-Nakao has worked as general staff nurse in obstetrics and gynecology, as home visiting nurse, and as a certified lactation educator for the past six years.

I also extend thanks to the following people:

Sleep information contributor Dr. Alexander Golbin, who is leading the study of sleep medicine in the country.

Experienced chef contributors Mee Kim Chavez, Laurel Erickson, Ghislaine Guigon, Anthurla Kapos, Tasia Koliopoulos, Susan Klimala, Rachel Jones, Lambrini Linardakis, Cyndia Cayias, Emila Linardakis, Ernestine Pippas, Nancy Melander,

Greg Mori, Angelina Nepolis, Sophia Nepolis, Antigone Polite, Nitsa Tsoutsounakis, Carol Wootton, and Pam Zoumadakis for their demonstration of great fatherhood and motherhood.

To the project team at Prima, Lorna Eby, and Michelle McCormack, whose insatiable need for quality would not let them release this book until it was perfect.

And to Sophia, my sister, whose cooking will be hard to beat; to Dr. Mary Cadieux, professor of *in vitro* fertilization, University of Washington, for her support on this book; and to nutritionist Rachel Jones, M.S., University of California at Berkeley, who contributed a professional evaluation.

And most of all to you, the reader. May this book prove a useful resource for you and your growing babies.

INTRODUCTION

Have you ever seen the 1987 movie *Baby Boom* starring Diane Keaton, who portrays an aggressive and ambitious career woman who finds her life irrevocably changed when a baby arrives? This hilarious comedy contains a lot of truth, especially when Keaton's character decides to leave the corporate job, corner office, and politics behind to make gourmet baby food from her barn in Vermont.

This book is the culmination of over three years of development and is a guide for new parents who want to provide a quality option to the current factory-bottled products. Many of today's parents share the values and dilemmas of Keaton's character—they want to cook for their newborn while giving 110% to a job or other commitment that takes up most of their day. Where do those raising a helpless infant go to find recipes for freshly prepared baby foods? Only a handful of books are available, most of which are rather dry reading.

At last, *Homemade Baby Food Pure & Simple* is here to help you!

The idea for this book was conceived right after my first book, *Recipes Sworn to Secrecy,* was completed. After ten successful years climbing the human resources career ladder, while occupying the vice-president's chair at a large corporation, I began thinking about having my own children. Two more working years passed, during which I continued to cull and revise my baby food recipes, before I decided to concentrate on having children, taking care of my husband's needs, and spending time with my aging mother. While anticipating my child's birth, I prepared balanced recipes for babies in their growing months. I provide recipes in this book for parents who wish to create healthy homemade baby foods as an alternative to the more common commercially prepared foods.

What you're holding in your hands is essentially a cookbook designed to provide easy-to-make recipes, accurate information, and advice from nationally recognized physicians and consultants. My husband, Dr. Nikos Linardakis, is a physician and medical editor/author of twelve books published by McGraw-Hill. Dr. Linardakis contributes his expertise in this book. Stephanie Mori-Nakao R.N., B.S.N, and C.L.E (certified lactation educator) provides very important information on breastfeeding and formula feeding. Nutritionist Rachel Jones, M.S., contributes her nutritional experience. You will also reap the benefit of recipes and advice from "experienced chefs"—mothers from around the United States who have made their own baby food.

Getting the Most Out of This Book

Because the book is designed to take you through the feeding stages of your growing baby, you will gain the most by working from the beginning through each chapter. Chapter 1, Why Make Your Own Natural Baby Food?, gives the reasons why today's parents make or buy baby food and looks at the pros and cons of each way of feeding your infant. You'll learn how to read and understand food labels and what to look for in prepared baby foods ingredients.

Chapter 2, Breast, Bottle, or Both?, discusses the benefits of breastfeeding, bottlefeeding, and a mixture of the two.

Chapter 3, Nutrition for Infants and Toddlers, is an extensive chapter in which we study six categories of nutrients—carbohydrates, fats, minerals, protein, vitamins, and water—and their sources. Here you'll learn about each important mineral and the recommended daily allowances.

Chapter 4, Starting Solids, points out that most babies start eating solids at four months; therefore parents must understand what to feed and especially what *not* to feed their babies at this time. Starting Solids discusses what signs to look for when your baby is ready to begin solids and which foods to start with.

Chapter 5, Preparing Homemade Baby Food, covers the basic equipment you'll need to cook your baby foods and explores the preparing, freezing, and storing of baby food.

Chapter 6, The Best Food for Babies: Beginner Recipes, identifies the best foods and assists parents with beginners' recipes. Recipes target babies from the age of four months to approximately six months and include healthy ingredients such as meat and poultry, vegetables and fruits, cereals and grains, and vegetable and fruit purees.

Chapter 7, More of the Best Foods: Intermediate Recipes, is intended for babies from seven months through twelve months.

Chapter 8, Recipes from Experienced Chefs and Parents, includes recipes and expert advice from experienced mothers and fathers in the United States. These nutritional recipes are categorized by age to assist you in deciding when it's appropriate to introduce each of them.

Chapter 9, Recipes for a Toddler's Family, suggests that parents offer children the opportunity to explore international flavors with their taste buds. Recipes that the whole family can enjoy are categorized by country. Don't worry, the American section still contains many favorites such as Baked Apples and Fruit Juice Pops!

Chapter 10, Recipes for Restlessness and Allergies, includes recipes for the allergy-sensitive child and recipes that contain foods that help your child sleep.

Chapter 11, Making Seasonal, Holiday, and Birthday Foods Fun, will walk you through each season and the joys that come with having a family. Here you'll find recipes for any time of year, as well as ideas for planning parties, including games and themes for birthday and other celebrations.

Chapter 12, Recipes for Homemade Craft and Baby Supplies, continues the concept of having fun in your kitchen, but rather than focusing on food, it offers tips and recipes for preparing inedible but practical items such as play dough, finger paint, baby wipes, and oils.

The appendices provide information on breastfeeding, a section that includes books and Web pages that are excellent information sources for parents, and a weights and measures section that lists several conversion charts to help you with measuring and cooking.

I am honored that you have decided to purchase this book for your family, whether as a gift or as a resource to help you make your own baby food. Let's have some fun following *Homemade Baby Food Pure & Simple*!

CHAPTER 1

Why Make Your Own Natural Baby Food?

There is no sincerer love than the love of food.
—George Bernard Shaw

Jennifer turned her cart down the baby food aisle of the grocery store. Her heart skipped a beat and she smiled to herself, thinking that this was the first time she'd been here with a purpose. Her baby was due in a month and she had never before paid close attention to this aisle full of tiny jars, boxes, canisters, and plenty of diapers. She first stopped at the bins of tiny jars—they were so cute! Applesauce, carrots, peach cobbler, vegetable beef dinner—good heavens, there were so many, where was she supposed to start?

She picked up a jar and read the label. What were all those long, hard-to-say ingredients doing in there? "Does my baby need those things? Probably not the modified food starch or salt," she speculated. Some were vitamins, she could tell, but what were those other chemical-sounding things? Would they hurt her precious baby? She saw a date stamped on the top that wasn't until late the following year. "My goodness, how fresh is this?" she wondered.

Some of the mixed foods didn't sound too appetizing, all cooked and blended together. "Hmm, wonder what they taste like," she pondered. She wasn't as excited as she had been when she first turned down the aisle.

Then she glanced up and saw boxes of baby cereal and bottles of baby juice. Did her child really need those items? Were they good, or would her baby be better off without them?

Then she started noticing prices. Not bad, she thought. Some little jars of food were three for a dollar; others were sixty-nine cents a piece. She could afford that—but wait, how much of these would her baby be eating and for how long? Those costs could add up quickly. "This could get expensive," she realized.

Soon Jennifer's mind was overwhelmed by choices and spinning with indecision—which to feed first, whether to even feed these foods to her baby. She left the aisle realizing she'd better get more information—and fast. Even though she planned to breastfeed, she knew it wouldn't be long before she'd need to know more about feeding her first child.

When you bring your baby home from the hospital, one of the first things you start worrying about is whether or not your new bundle of love is getting enough to eat. Usually this concern is groundless, but you worry anyway. Then the baby grows and thrives and sits up . . . and wants more to eat. Before you know it, you've reached another milestone—it's time to introduce solids into the diet.

Many parents start their babies on cereal. Very quickly, though, it's time to add more foods to your child's diet. This is when you start thinking seriously about types of baby food. Should you make it yourself or buy it? Is there really a difference? The answer is yes, there is a big difference.

Choosing the right food. As a busy, first-time parent, you'll probably lean toward prepared food—especially with creative marketing influencing your daily decision to open another jar of pureed peas. Companies compete heavily for new parents' brand loyalty and business. As you're strolling down the baby food aisle in a supermarket, impressive advertising campaigns will pressure and reassure you to buy their food. Gerber, for example, advertises its foods as a reasonable choice with the hard-to-resist slogan, "For learning to eat smart, right from the start."

What you may not know. More than 40 percent of the cost of prepared baby food, according to the American Marketing Association, goes into packaging, labor, advertising, and overhead. Magazines for parents are filled with ads that feature smiling, healthy babies and the foods they eat. Marketing departments

> Today's parents spend almost three times as much of their income on baby food as their own parents did. First births drive new purchases, and parents spend 5 to 15 percent more on their first child.

are quick to pick up on trends, such as consumer preferences and the use of catchy words like "natural" and "organic." But beware: Such words, printed on a jar of baby food, may be misleading, since they are primarily meant to sell the product by convincing parents that what their child will be consuming is wholesome and nutritious.

The four factors. It's true that most babies raised on commercially prepared food do thrive. Nevertheless, when deciding whether to choose ready-made or homemade food, you need to consider four factors: nutritional value, cost, taste, and your own process of bonding with your child.

Nutritional Value

What's your baby eating? The nutritional superiority of home-made baby food is the best reason to make your own. Commercial baby foods, like most prepared foods, may be overrefined, overprocessed, full of additives, and far from "natural." Many contain starch, sugar, and salt. The starch is used as a thickening agent and to help keep the food from separating. Although starch is not necessarily harmful, it acts as a filler, diluting the otherwise nutrient-rich food.

The not-so-obvious additives. Sugars, such as corn syrup, dextrose, and sucrose, are added to enhance flavor. Sugars are devoid of nutrients, providing virtually no nutritional value except calories. Finally, the added salt enhances taste and acts as a preservative. Babies do have an innate desire for sweetness, but not for salt. Because their taste for salt has not yet been acquired, babies don't need it added to their food.

Destroying nutrients. In addition, the light in well-lit supermarkets may shine through the clear glass jars and destroy nutrients, such as the B vitamin riboflavin. You should also note whether the jars are stored in direct sunlight, which can also destroy certain nutrients.

Homemade nutrition. Your homemade baby food won't be stored in clear jars where light can deplete its nutrients. You won't need to add any starch, sugar, or salt. And you can also make sure that the produce you use is washed free of any traces of pesticides or other potentially harmful substances (see the sidebar "Washing Fresh Produce" on page 5). If you're concerned about quality, this book will lead you to feel confident that your child is getting the best foods possible.

Washing Fresh Produce

Are you concerned about removing pesticides in the fresh produce you buy? If so, you have two options. The method recommended by most health professionals is to scrub produce under briskly running water. A soft brush, along with the force of the water, will help remove harmful bacteria, pesticides, and other chemical residues. Some people may consider purchasing fruit and vegetable washes. These products are only slightly more effective than a good scrubbing under briskly running water. However, if you want to try them, I recommend one called VegiWash and another called Fit. You'll find VegiWash at most natural-food stores or through the company's Web site (www.vegiwash .com), and Fit is available in your local grocery store.

Reading Food Labels

If you choose to buy baby food, you'll need to understand how to read the food labels so you can make the best food choices for your baby.

Understand what you're reading. The Food and Drug Administration (FDA) regulates the labeling of all baby foods with the exception of strained meats (this labeling is controlled by the U.S. Department of Agriculture). The FDA requires that labeling on infant food (for babies under a year old) list more nutrients than do labels on other foods. When checking labels on baby foods, pay particularly close attention to the following:

- *Additives:* The fewer artificial preservatives, additives, and colorings, the better. Choose products with little or no salt and sugar. The further down on the ingredient list an item is, the less of it there is in the product.
- *Water content:* Commercially prepared food often contains water added for processing. The more water, the more diluted the food.
- *100 percent natural:* Sugar, salt, and starch are "natural" because they're not artificially made chemicals. But you still don't want your baby eating much of these, so don't be swayed by this label claim. Check carefully for ingredients you prefer to avoid.
- *Starch content:* Try to choose foods that have little or no starch added—it just fills up baby without offering much in the way of nutrients.
- *Nutritional facts panel:* Check for percentages of daily recommended allowances of vitamins and minerals. Compare products and choose ones that have higher percentages. For instance, in comparing a jar of baby food peaches to peach cobbler, you'll see that the peaches contain more vitamin A and potassium than the cobbler. (The cobbler, on the other hand, will likely contain starch and sugar.) Always compare similar products and choose the one with the highest nutrient content.
- *Ingredients:* Make sure there are no ingredients to which your baby is allergic, and that all ingredients are age appropriate. For example, don't choose a "dinner" containing meat for a six-month-old, as meats should not be introduced until about nine months or later. (See page 26 for a list of what to feed your baby when.)

How Much Food Is Enough?

It's one thing to know which foods to feed your baby, but an often-asked question is "How much?" The general rule of thumb is that a "serving" of most solid foods is one tablespoon per year of age (up to one-half cup), and two ounces for meat or meat alternates, although a baby may eat more than one serving of a food at any given meal.

Listen to your baby. The most important guideline to keep in mind is to pay attention to what your baby tells you. She'll let you know when she's hungry and will turn her head away repeatedly when she's full. In order for children to grow up without feeding problems, they must be able to recognize and pay attention to their own internal cues for hunger and fullness. If these are constantly overridden, such as by an overexuberant parent, the child learns not to trust or listen to the internal cue. That can set the stage for an eating disorder later in life. So when baby's done eating, respect that and don't force more food—she'll learn to trust herself, trust you, and trust the world, feeling that it is a safe place to be that responds to her needs.

Follow a plan. Below is a chart that gives you a rough idea of the average calorie needs of babies at different ages, plus a sample menu plan.

Recommended Dietary Allowances for Calorie Needs of Infants and Young Children

Age	Daily Calories	
0 to 6 months	650	
6 to 12 months	850	(continues on next page)

(continued from page 7)

1 to 3 years	1,300
4 to 6 years	1,800
7 to 10 years	2,000

Use a menu. To help you better understand the calorie amounts in various foods that might make up an infant's daily diet, here are samples of potential daily menus.

Caloric Value of Sample Daily Menu for Four- to Six-Month-Old

Food	Calories
20 fluid ounces formula (4 bottles at 5 ounces each)	500
2 tablespoons iron-fortified infant cereal	33
1 tablespoon mashed banana	7
2 tablespoons vegetables	10
1 tablespoon well-cooked, mashed legumes	50
2 ounces juice (apple or carrot)	60
Total Calories	**660**

Caloric Value of Sample Daily Menu for Nine- to Twelve-Month-Old

Food	Calories
16 fluid ounces formula or human milk throughout the day	400

Breakfast	
Milk or formula	(see previous)
3 tablespoons iron-fortified baby cereal	50
2 tablespoons mashed banana	14
Morning Snack	
¼ cup yogurt	36
1 tablespoon fruit	7
Lunch	
Milk or formula	(see previous)
3 tablespoons noodles	40
2 tablespoons vegetables	10
1 egg yolk or ¼ cup tofu	55
Afternoon Snack	
Milk or formula	(see previous)
½ slice toast	35
½ tablespoon thinned peanut butter	48
Dinner	
Milk or formula	(see previous)
2 ounces chopped meat or well-cooked, mashed legumes	125
2 tablespoons potato, rice, or pasta	24
2 tablespoons vegetables	10
2 tablespoons fruit	14
Total Calories	**868**

Cost

Baby food is a $1.25-billion-a-year industry in the United States. Three national brands—Gerber, Beech-Nut, and Heinz—control more than 95 percent of the market. Their marketing and packaging costs are built into the price you pay for a jar of baby food. Compared to making your baby food fresh, commercial baby food has no "in" season; therefore, it's virtually never on sale (unless it's nearing the "sell by" date, after which you can't be sure of the quality).

The frugal way. If you make your baby food, you'll find it more cost-effective for several reasons. First, you can look for sales and buy produce in season. Consider, for example, the cost of buying commercially prepared green peas compared with the cost of preparing them yourself. A 2½-ounce jar costs approximately 39 cents. That's 15.6 cents per ounce. If you buy frozen peas and cook and mash them, you'll pay approximately 8.1 cents per ounce. Organically grown frozen peas will cost slightly more.

You really are saving money. The cost of commercially prepared baby food is almost double that of homemade. If you look at the following chart, you'll see that you can achieve similar savings with other foods—typically between 40 percent and 100 percent.

Deciding Whether to Make or Buy Baby Food

	Commercial Baby Food	Homemade Baby Food
Variety	Variety is limited to store buyer's selection	Variety is unlimited. You control your baby's choices

Safety	You can be assured that jars have been sterilized. However, jars may be on shelves for a long time (check expiration date)	You have total control over the sterilization of your baby's food and jars and that the food is fresh
Added Ingredients	Some companies add salt and artificial colors and flavors to baby food	You can add the necessary nutrients your baby needs and keep additives out of the diet
Preparation	Limited preparation is needed	Preparing the initial batch of food takes time. After that, very little preparation is needed
Storage	Some companies vacuum seal their food. Be sure to check labels for expiration dates	You store food in freezer or refrigerator
Cost	Less expensive for foods that are not in season	Can be up to 40 percent less expensive than prepared baby food and is less expensive as a rule
Nutrition	Depends on how the food was prepared and stored	Hints for maximizing nutrients: Don't overcook, cover boiling foods, purchase the right appliances such as a steamer and food processor

Jennifer went to the library and checked out a book about making baby food. She was excited to find out how easy it was—just put a little cooked food in the blender and it's ready. She realized that those three jars for $1 weren't such a bargain, when all she needed to do was blend some of the family's broccoli before adding anything to it—that would just cost pennies—and be really fresh!

Taste

You may think you'll buy commercially prepared baby food because it tastes good. With just a little time, understanding, and research, though, you may find the opposite is true.

Taste test. Have you ever sampled commercial baby food? Try it! Most commercially prepared baby food is bland. When foods get watered down and have fillers such as starch added, the rich, natural taste of the food is lost. Flavor enhancers such as salt and sugar are added, but the taste just isn't the same.

Homemade taste. You'll soon see what I mean about the taste advantage of making your own baby food. If you use fresh ingredients, the flavor will be so robust you won't even feel the need to add salt or sugar.

Bonding with Your Child

Whatever the quality of the product they turn out, large baby food manufacturers cannot prepare food with the same "love and attention" that you put into it, because you do it just for your own child.

Taking the time. Most of all, if you prepare the food yourself, you know exactly what goes into it. So you may ask: How can I bond with my child simply by preparing his food? You, as a parent, will gain a higher level of self-esteem, accomplishment, and ability to care for your child, as well as learn his personal tastes and add a loving touch to his food.

Preparing the food with love. Your child will bond with you by hearing kitchen sounds that will become familiar, smelling aromas that may later trigger fond memories, and experiencing favorite family foods. And, if you're employed outside your home, making the food in advance is a way of giving your baby some love while you are away.

Having fun. Making baby food takes little time and minimal effort. Whether you use a fancy food processor, a simple blender, or a wire mesh strainer with a spoon, it will be fun to do (see chapter 5 for a discussion of equipment that will work well for you).

Keeping it simple. Using easy storage methods, you can easily prepare food weeks in advance without much hassle. The tips here will be especially helpful to excited first-time parents—even those who may be nervous about preparing their own foods!

Jennifer talked to some of the mothers at her birthing class who already had children. "Making your own baby food is easy and cheap," several told her.

"Plus," added another mother, "this may sound silly, but it has your own love and energy in it—and I think that makes a difference."

Jennifer was sold—she was going to learn how to make food for her baby without depending on the store-bought kind. "I can keep just a few of those in the cupboard," she decided, "for when things get really hectic. But my baby's going to have the best, and it's going to be from me!"

CHAPTER 2

Breast, Bottle, or Both?

"Enjoy the beauty of creation and preserve it."
—Maelou T., from the book *Love, From Grandma*,
compiled by Becky L. Amble

A ngela woke at about 3:00 A.M. to her newborn daughter, Ashley's, soft cries. She peered into the bassinet next to her bed and smiled at the little bundle. She lifted Ashley into her arms, crawled back beneath the warm covers, and cradled her while she nursed on one side then the other. The nightlight offered just enough glow that she could stare in wonder at Ashley's tiny features while she held her close. Before long the baby was done and satisfied. Angela placed her carefully back into the bassinet and they both settled down to go back to sleep. "How easy," Angela thought. "Very little crying, no fuss, not much lost sleep—people who complain about nighttime feedings must use bottles," she mused, as sleep overcame her again.

Until your baby is between four to six months old, breast milk or formula will be his sole source of nutrition. You'll probably decide while you're pregnant whether to go with breastfeeding or bottlefeeding. Consider your decision carefully, though, because it has implications for both you and your baby. Here are some facts to keep in mind as you make your decision on breast-feeding versus formula-feeding.

What's the Difference?

First you need to consider the differences between breast milk and formula. Most formulas are derived either from cow's milk or soybeans. (Regular, unmodified cow's milk should not be given to infants younger than one year.) Since 1980, formula manufacturers have been required to adhere to strict guidelines for quality and nutrient composition as set by federal law.

Protein

The risks of cow's milk. Cow's milk must be modified because its protein content is too high for baby: 20 percent of calories versus only 7 percent of the calories in breast milk. Not only is the protein so concentrated that it could tax an infant's kidneys, but its major type of protein, casein, forms a tough, hard-to-digest curd in the infant's stomach.

    The benefits of breast milk. Breast milk is easier for baby to digest because its major form of protein is whey, which contains lactalbumin. Lactalbumin forms soft, easy-to-digest curds. Most infant formulas try to mimic the proportions and type of protein found in breast milk. The casein is heat-treated for easier digestibility and some manufacturers add extra whey since it is so easy to digest.

Carbohydrates

Why carbohydrates are important. Carbohydrates provide 42 percent of the calories in breast milk and only 30 percent of the calories in cow's milk. For that reason, formulas with a cow's milk base must have some form of carbohydrate supplements.

Using lactose. Lactose is the most common carbohydrate used. Lactose is a naturally occurring sugar found in milk. Some formulas are made with corn syrup for the carbohydrate; these are useful for babies who are lactose intolerant, meaning they cannot digest lactose, however you should only use corn syrup in special situations, as it can cause botulism.

Fats

Both breast milk and formula derive about 50 percent of their calories from fat—necessary for proper brain and nerve development of the infant.

What is in the milk? Monounsaturated fat is predominant in both types of milk, but human milk gets about 4 percent of its calories from essential fatty acids. Essential fatty acids are fats the body cannot make, therefore must be obtained from food. Unmodified cow's milk, on the other hand, gets only 1 percent of its calories from this important nutrient.

Modified milk. Many formulas start with nonfat cow's milk and add vegetable oils so that absorption is similar to that of human milk, but essential fatty acid content is lacking compared to that of human milk.

What are you getting? Vegetable oils contain adequate amounts of the essential fat called linoleic acid, otherwise known as omega-6, but very little, if any, linolenic acid (omega-

3), which plays an important role in brain development. Research indicates that mother's milk is a better source of the essential fatty acid called omega-3 than formula. It's expensive to add omega-3 fats to formula, but because of its importance, some manufacturers may do so.

You are what you eat. Your breast milk will reflect the type of fat you eat—if you eat a diet high in unhealthful saturated fats, that type of fat will increase in your milk as well. If you are nursing, you should eat fats that are mostly monounsaturated, such as olive and canola oils, and limit animal fats that are high in saturated fat. Two or three servings of fish each week will help ensure that there is plenty of omega-3 fats for you and your baby.

Minerals and Vitamins

The mineral and vitamin content of breast milk also differs from that of cow's milk.

What is your baby getting—and is it safe? Unmodified cow's milk contains more calcium, phosphorus, sodium, potassium, and fluoride than does breast milk. This high concentration of minerals can damage a baby's kidneys, so formula makers adjust the mineral content to be closer to that of human milk. One thing they can't control though, is the bioavailability of minerals.

Understanding bioavailability. Bioavailablity refers to how well the body is able to absorb and use a certain nutrient. The iron and zinc in human milk are much more bioavailable; baby can absorb and use them much more efficiently than the same minerals found in formula. For instance, there are only about three milligrams of iron per quart of breast milk or formula. But babies absorb 49 percent of the iron coming from breast milk, but less than 1 percent of the iron in formula.

Playing dentist. Fluoride, a mineral that helps to strengthen teeth and bones, may need to be given as a supplement to breastfed infants, as very little of the mother's fluoride passes into the breast milk.

Providing baby with vitamins. Breast milk also contains higher levels of vitamin E than formula, and both milks contain adequate vitamin A—two of the fat-soluble vitamins. Human milk has less of the fat-soluble vitamin D than does cow's milk because cow's milk is usually fortified with 400 international units (IU) per quart while mother's milk contributes only about 40 to 50 IU per quart. For this reason, breastfed infants may need supplements of vitamin D as they get older in order to form strong bones. The last fat-soluble vitamin, K, is usually not of concern. Many infants are given an injection of the vitamin at birth, which tides them over until the bacteria in their intestines starts to make adequate amounts of the vitamin.

Water-soluble vitamins. The water-soluble vitamins, which include vitamin C and all the B vitamins, are reflective of the nursing mother's intake. A well-nourished mother will supply adequate amounts of these vitamins in her milk. Formula manufacturers add enough of these vitamins to meet babies' needs.

Advantages of Breastfeeding

Natalie walked out of her doctor's office feeling blue. Her baby was due any day now and the lactation nurse had pressured her again about breastfeeding. Natalie knew there were certain things breast milk had that formula couldn't give her baby, but she wasn't sure she could do it. She knew she would feel uncomfortable doing it in public and she was afraid of all those stories her girlfriends told her about letdown or milk dripping through their clothes. "That nurse doesn't understand my side," she thought tearfully, as she made her way to the car. The nurse had finally let up a little and suggested that maybe Natalie could nurse for just the first week, when she wouldn't be going out, so that her baby could still get some of her special antibodies. Natalie thought she might be able to do that so decided to think about it.

Both mother and child reap multiple benefits from breastfeeding. Carefully consider the following information as you make your decision whether to nurse your baby or use formula.

Advantages for Baby

Breastfeeding benefits babies in several ways.

The nutritionally superior choice. As discussed in the previous section, formulas try to mimic mother's breast milk, but don't quite make the grade. For instance, the bioavailability of iron cannot be duplicated in formula and omega-3 fats may be lacking. The American Academy of Pediatrics states that "Human milk is uniquely superior for infant feeding."

Enhancing the immune system. Both colostrum (the first milk to appear, yellowish in color) and mature breast milk contain immune factors. They are especially rich in one called immunoglobulin A or IgA for short. These provide the infant with immunity from some diseases, helping to compensate for baby's immature immune system. Breastfeeding also supplies the infant with *Lactobacillus bifidus* factor. This substance encourages growth of *Lactobacillus bifidus* bacteria and other beneficial bacteria in the intestinal tract. At the same time, it creates an acidic environment that limits the growth of potentially harmful bacteria that could cause diarrhea. The presence of beneficial bacteria and easily digested milk give the stools of a breastfed baby a less offensive odor than those of a bottlefed baby. Research indicates that to get the full benefit of these immune enhancers, nursing needs to continue for at least three months, but some benefit is received even if baby only gets the colostrum.

Lessening allergies and intolerances. Breastfeeding reduces the incidence of allergies in babies and avoids the possibility of infants developing intolerances to different formulas. Cow's milk–derived formulas contain a number of potentially allergy-causing proteins, as do soy-based formulas. If your family has a history of allergies, breastfeeding your infant is strongly recommended because of the immune antibodies breast milk provides.

Ensures against overfeeding. The amount of mother's milk produced is in direct response to demand from the baby. The more or less suckling that occurs, the more or less milk the breasts make, providing the baby with just the right amount.

Proper jaw and tooth development. The position and actions of the tongue, mouth, and jaw that occur while baby is sucking the human nipple is just right for proper oral development. Baby bottle manufacturers try to imitate Mother Nature, but none are quite the same.

A fresh and safe approach. Mother's milk is certainly fresh, and there's no fear of contamination from harmful bacteria that may be found in previously used bottles and around the kitchen.

Making SIDS (sudden infant death syndrome) less likely. The link is not completely clear, but researchers hypothesize that certain bacteria may be responsible for SIDS. Since breastfed babies receive immune boosters through breast milk, they appear to be better able to fight off the lethal bacteria.

Milk Causes Ear Infections?

When babies are put to bed with a bottle, it's easy for formula to pool in the mouth and flow into the eustachian tube, which opens into the throat from the middle ear. The formula provides a food source for bacteria that cause ear infections. Breastfed babies obviously do not sleep with a bottle in their mouths so they are less prone to this uncomfortable affliction.

"Hey Natalie, do you have the baby's food?" her husband quipped, as he loaded the car with even more baby items. This first family-reunion picnic with the new baby was a big event.

"You bet," Natalie shot back, patting her chest. "Right here, all ready to go—clean, fresh, and made-to-order!"

Advantages for the Mother

Breastfeeding benefits mothers in several ways.

Toning the uterus. Every time baby nurses the hormone oxytocin is produced. Oxytocin enables the "let-down" reflex (milk flow) in the breasts, but also stimulates the muscle cells of the uterus to contract. Lactation immediately after delivery can help shut down the bleeding of the uterus, and over time will help it return to normal size.

Losing the pregnancy pounds. Nursing moms usually have a large appetite, and rightly so. A mother needs to eat about 500 more calories per day than when she was not pregnant to make sufficient milk. It takes a total of about 750 calories per day for the body to make adequate milk for one baby. The additional 150 calories come from using up body fat laid down during pregnancy just for this purpose. As most new moms nurse their babies, they'll more easily lose those fat pads and return to pre-pregnancy weight.

Breast milk is free. No need to buy formula, just keep mother well nourished!

Experiencing close mother-child contact. Breastfeeding is a natural extension of pregnancy in that the mother's body continues to nourish the infant. In addition, close physical contact helps babies thrive. The emotional contact that happens during each feeding also contributes toward the strong bond that develops between mother and baby.

A convenient option. The new mother doesn't need to spend time washing bottles and preparing formulas, thus has more time to spend with her baby. Breast milk is already "prepared" and sterile. While you may need to find a private place to nurse, it's easier than lugging bottles of formula and worrying about keeping them cold or having to warm them for feeding.

Advantages of Breastfeeding

1. Breast milk is ready to feed and always at the right temperature
2. There's no bottle to wash or heat
3. It's chemically made just for your baby
4. It keeps your baby well with an immunity against illness
5. It protects baby's bowels from parasites
6. It's easy for baby to digest
7. It increases mother–infant bonding
8. It saves in costs (up to $140 to $160 per month)
9. Most moms return to health quicker and lose weight quicker than non-breastfeeding moms.

As Angela experienced in the beginning of the chapter, it's easy to nurse your baby—no fuss, no mess—especially at night.

Keeping mother healthy. A nursing mother just needs adequate calories (this is *not* the time for dieting!) as well as about three to four quarts of water—to produce enough high-quality milk for her baby to gain at least one ounce a day. Drinking those twelve to sixteen cups of water is important in order to be able to consistently make the amount of milk baby needs.

CHAPTER 3

Nutrition for Infants and Toddlers

You don't have to cook fancy or complicated masterpieces—just good food from fresh ingredients.
—Julia Child

*M*arcia works at a WIC clinic—the federal Women, Infants and Children program that supplies formula and certain foods (such as milk and low-sugar cereals) to limited-income families with children under age five. She teaches nutrition basics to the many mothers she sees each day. Most of them are eager to learn how to nourish their babies well, and after a series of lessons, some will tell Marcia, "You've changed my life— you've changed the way I feed my family. Thank you!" Marcia loves getting mothers and babies on the right path to eating healthful food.

A few words on nutrition before we get started: As a new parent, you need to know some basics about nourishing your child.

Act now and keep your baby healthy. A healthful diet is not something that your baby, soon to be a child, can get later. Babies grow faster during the first year than at any other time in life. A healthy, growing baby needs the same collection of nutrients as an adult, but in smaller amounts. The six principal categories of nutrients are carbohydrates, fats, proteins, vitamins, minerals, and water. (You may not think of water as a nutrient, but it's essential for life, therefore is considered a nutrient.)

Carbohydrates

Carbohydrates come in the form of sugar, starch, and fiber.

Some other forms of carbohydrates. Sugars are considered simple carbohydrates; they digest very quickly. Starches are complex carbohydrates, meaning they have a more complex structure, which takes longer to digest. Fiber is the indigestible portion of foods—found only in foods from plant sources.

What do carbohydrates do? Carbohydrates provide calories for energy that are important for a baby's physical activity, brain, and nervous system. Carbohydrates also help the body utilize stored fats.

Giving your baby starches. Starch sources that are good to introduce first to babies are the iron-fortified cereals mentioned earlier. As baby starts to eat vegetables, starchy ones to include are peas, corn, and potatoes, although all vegetables are good sources of carbohydrates.

Giving your baby sugars. Fruits such as apples, bananas, plums, peaches, and pears provide simple sugars. Simple sugars also include added table sugar (sucrose), brown sugar, and corn syrup. Babies don't need these added sugars and they should be used only sparingly even with children.

Fats

Fats are essential for the developing child.

What do fats do? Fats provide the body with reserve energy stores; the fat-soluble vitamins A, D, E, and K; as well as the essential fats the body cannot make. Essential fatty acids must be obtained from the diet. They are important to your baby's growth and development as well as healthy skin.

Some other forms of fats. The essential fatty acids are linoleic acid, linolenic acid, and sometimes arachidonic acid. Of these, linoleic acid is the most important because, under the right conditions, the body can transform it into arachidonic acid. Examples of foods containing some or all of these essential fatty acids include breast milk, vegetable oils, especially canola oil and flaxseed oils, meats, fish, soybean products, and avocados. Nuts are rich in fatty acids, too, but wait until your child is older before serving these. Once your baby is over ten months old, she will get more of these fats as you include a variety of foods in her meals. Please review the following food introduction chart for more details.

Introducing Solids in the First Year of Baby's Life

Food	Age (in months)	Problems (if any)
Pureed food	8	
Slightly textured food	12	
Apple juice	4 to 6	
Applesauce	4 to 6	
Avocado	4 to 6	
Banana	4 to 6	
Barley	4 to 6	
Beets	8	
Berries	12	allergies

Broccoli	7	
Brussels sprouts	8	
Butter as an ingredient (1 teaspoon per 16 ounces)	10	
Cabbage	8	
Carrots	7	
Chicken	8	
Cottage cheese	7	
Egg white	12	allergies
Egg yolk	8	
Fish (all boneless, skinless)		
Whitefish	10	
Salmon	10	
Bass	10	
Trout	10	
Halibut	10	
Shellfish	12	allergies
Greenbeans	8	
Honey	12	botulism
Milk (cow's)	12	allergies
Nuts (in purees)	12	allergies/choking hazards
Oats	4 to 6	
Orange juice	12	digestion
Papaya	4 to 6	
Peaches	4 to 6	

(continues next page)

(continued from page 27)

Peanut butter (thinned)	8	
Pears	4 to 6	
Pear juice	4 to 6	
Peas	4 to 6	
Potatoes	4 to 6	
Rice (brown)	8	
Rice (white)	7	
Spinach	8	
Squash	7	
Sweet potato	4 to 6	
Tofu	8 to 12	
Tomato	12	digestion
Wheat	7 to 12	allergies
Yogurt	7	
Zucchini	7	

Heart smart from the start. Nutritionists recommend low-fat, low-cholesterol diets for children over the age of about two to five, anticipating that this will help establish healthy eating habits and reduce their risk of heart disease later in life.

Fat is important. Babies need dietary fat to form cholesterol in the body—a major component of brain cells, nerves, and the fatty sheath around their nerves. Cholesterol is not only an essential constituent of body tissues, but is also required for the regulation of important body functions. We don't need to worry about consuming cholesterol, however, because our bodies readily synthesize it from fat, especially saturated fat.

Protein

What does protein do? Protein is made up of building blocks called amino acids. Breast milk supplies the baby with the ideal mixture of these amino acids although formula makers attempt to mimic the composition of breast milk.

Some other forms of protein. The protein in both breast milk and formula is in a form more easily digested than that found in regular cow's milk. You can introduce other types of protein at around six to eight months of age. Other proteins include poultry, meats, egg yolks, and cooked, pureed dry beans. Avoid shellfish and egg whites until after the first year. Tofu is a good source of protein, but make sure your baby is not allergic to it—you might want to wait until the one-year mark before serving this food, too.

Giving your baby protein. Infants and toddlers only need thirteen to sixteen grams of protein each day. This amount is very easy to get because of their breast milk or formula intake, both of which are rich protein sources. Cow's milk, which your toddler can drink, is also high in protein.

Protein

Recommended dietary allowances:

Infants 6 months to 1 year: 14 grams

Toddlers 1 to 3 years: 16 grams

Importance of protein: Maintains and builds body tissue and is therefore critical to a growing child. It also supplies part of the baby's daily energy requirements.

Good sources of protein: Pureed meat, fish, poultry, eggs, peanut butter, dairy products, and tofu.

How Much Fat and Cholesterol?

The National Cholesterol Education Program recommends the following amounts for everyone over two years of age, although a child can gradually work toward these goals after the age of two and attain them by the age of five:

Total maximum fat intake: 30 percent of calorie intake (about 43 grams for toddlers*)
Saturated fats: 10 percent of calorie intake (about 14 grams for toddlers)
Monounsaturated fats: 10 percent of calorie intake (about 14 grams for toddlers)
Polyunsaturated fats: 10 percent of calorie intake (about 14 grams for toddlers)
Cholesterol: 300 milligrams per day *maximum*

*Generally speaking, children ages one through three are considered toddlers.

Minerals

What do minerals do? Minerals are elements contained in each cell of the body. Some minerals help body processes occur; others help transport substances, such as iron, to carry oxygen to the brain and muscles; and others provide structural support, such as calcium, phosphorous, and magnesium for bone formation.

Different forms of minerals. The most abundant minerals include calcium, phosphorus, magnesium, sulfur, potassium, sodium, and chloride. Minerals the body needs only in trace amounts include iron, zinc, iodine, selenium, copper, manganese, fluoride, chromium, and molybdenum.

Where to get your minerals. The following discussion lists major food sources of each of these minerals. Please refer to the nutritional guidelines chart on page 43 as to when they can be introduced to your baby. (As a general rule, they should be introduced in puree form.)

Calcium

Dietary reference intakes:

Infants 6 months to 1 year: 270 milligrams

Toddlers 1 to 3 years: 500 milligrams

Importance of calcium: Used for bone and tooth formation. Calcium is also critical for such vital functions as nerve conduction, muscle contraction, and blood clotting.

Good sources of calcium: Dairy products, dark green vegetables, dry beans, canned tomatoes, whole wheat flour, blackstrap molasses, tofu made with calcium salts, and fortified foods such as calcium-fortified orange juice and soymilk.

Phosphorus

Recommended dietary allowances:

Infants 6 months to 1 year: 275 milligrams

Toddlers 1 to 3 years: 460 milligrams

Importance of phosphorus: Together with calcium, phosphorus helps form bones and teeth. It also helps the body form the genetic material DNA and RNA, and thus is necessary for growth. In addition, it is an important part of cell membranes.

Good sources of phosphorus: Dairy products, meats, fish, dry beans, and whole grains. It is plentiful in foods so there is no need to worry about deficiencies.

Magnesium

Recommended dietary allowances:

Infants 6 months to 1 year: 75 milligrams

Toddlers 1 to 3 years: 80 milligrams

Importance of magnesium: Aids nerve and muscle functions, builds strong bones and teeth, and allows enzymes in the body to work properly.

Good sources of magnesium: Fruits and vegetables such as apples, citrus fruits, avocados, corn, and peas. Plus whole grains, dry beans, and soybean products.

Sodium

Estimated minimum requirements:

Infants 6 months to 1 year: 200 milligrams

Toddlers 1 to 3 years: 225 to 300 milligrams

Importance of sodium: Helps the body maintain fluid balance. Sodium works with potassium to bring water in and out of body cells. This mineral is also necessary for nerves to work properly.

Good sources of sodium: Unprocessed foods such as grains, fresh fruits, vegetables, meat, and dairy products contain small amounts of sodium. Table salt contributes a significant portion of sodium to the American diet, while processed and prepared foods yield the highest amounts. Healthy infants don't need more sodium than what is naturally available in their food sources. The food nutritional guidelines chart on page 43 will tell you when these foods should be introduced.

Potassium

Estimated minimum requirements:

Infants 6 months to 1 year: 700 milligrams

Toddlers 1 to 3 years: 1,000 to 1,400 milligrams

Importance of potassium: Works with sodium to maintain fluid balance in body cells. It helps regulate blood flow and works with magnesium in the synthesis of protein. It is considered a heart-healthy mineral because it helps regulate heartbeat and blood pressure. It's a good idea to get more of this mineral than the minimum listed above.

Good sources of potassium: In general, all fruits and vegetables. Rich sources include potatoes, spinach, cantaloupe, bananas, green leafy vegetables, citrus fruits, and dry beans.

Iron

Recommended dietary allowances:

Infants 6 months to 1 year: 10 milligrams

Toddlers 1 to 3 years: 10 milligrams

Importance of iron: Necessary for the proper formation of oxygen-rich red blood cells. At birth, an infant possesses body stores of iron sufficient to sustain red blood cell production for four to six months. If additional iron is not supplied after that time, progressive iron deficiency can occur. Iron-deficiency anemia (low blood iron levels) can lead to fatigue and long-term, possibly irreversible effects on the mental development of children. Iron carries oxygen in the bloodstream, and without enough oxygen the brain and muscles suffer.

Good sources of iron: Organ meats, red meat, poultry, fish, dry beans, dark green leafy vegetables, and enriched flour products such as bread.

One of the saddest problems Marcia faces in her daily work is iron-deficient babies. She knows that if babies don't get enough iron before the age of five, while their brain is undergoing a lot of development, their cognitive skills (learning, reasoning, and so on) never catch up to that of children who were not iron deficient. These children do less well in school than their nourished counterparts, even if they get enough iron during childhood. She tries to explain this to the many mothers she sees and tells them which foods baby should eat that are high in iron. Sadly, she finds that sometimes mothers deliberately withhold iron-rich foods from their babies so that they will be iron deficient—to avoid losing some of their food assistance package. Since some mothers don't understand the severity of the problem, Marcia tries to find other ways to get them the food they need so they won't feel the need to make their children iron deficient in order to keep receiving food assistance.

Zinc

Recommended dietary allowances:

Infants 6 months to 1 year: 5 milligrams

Toddlers 1 to 3 years: 10 milligrams

Importance of zinc: Helps many enzymes work properly, synthesizes DNA and RNA (genetic material cells need to reproduce), helps with vision and taste perception, and is a protector against infections and autoimmune disorders.

Good sources of zinc: Meats, fish, oysters, yogurt, whole grains, and dark, leafy greens.

Iodine

Recommended dietary allowances:

Infants 6 months to 1 year: 50 micrograms

Toddlers 1 to 3 years: 70 micrograms

Importance of iodine: Necessary for proper functioning of the thyroid gland and for normal reproduction.

Good sources of iodine: Seafood, iodized salt, dairy products, and bakery products (due to dough conditioners). Infants do not need more iodine than what is provided to them naturally in their food sources.

Manganese

Estimated safe and adequate daily dietary intakes:

Infants 6 months to 1 year: 0.6 to 1.0 milligram

Toddlers 1 to 3 years: 1.0 to 1.5 milligrams

Importance of manganese: Good for bone formation, for proper functioning of the central nervous system, for processing carbohydrates, and for reproduction.

Good sources of manganese: Whole grains, dry beans, nuts.

Selenium

Recommended dietary allowances:

Infants 6 months to 1 year: 15 micrograms

Toddlers 1 to 3 years: 20 micrograms

Importance of selenium: As an antioxidant, selenium protects cells and helps prevent cancer and heart disease—it works hand-in-hand with vitamin E. It also helps activate thyroid hormones, which regulate the body's rate of metabolism.

Good sources of selenium: Beef, fish, egg yolks, and shellfish, plus grains and seeds grown in selenium-rich soil.

Molybdenum

Estimated safe and adequate daily dietary intakes:

Infants 6 months to 1 year: 20 to 40 micrograms

Toddlers 1 to 3 years: 25 to 50 micrograms

Importance of molybdenum: This trace mineral is part of the enzyme that converts xanthine oxidase, which aids in the mobilization of iron from the liver.

Good sources of molybdenum: Dry beans, lentils, whole grains, nuts, and dark green, leafy vegetables.

Copper

Estimated safe and adequate daily dietary intakes:

Infants 6 months to 1 year: 0.6 to 0.7 milligram

Toddlers 1 to 3 years: 0.7 to 1.0 milligrams

Importance of copper: Needed for the formation of red blood cells and collagen. Collagen is the foundation of all body tissues from internal organs and bones to skin and teeth.

Good sources of copper: Meats, liver, dry beans, whole grains, raisins, and nuts. (Raisins and nuts should not be given to a child under two years old to avoid choking.)

Chromium

Estimated safe and adequate daily dietary intakes:

Infants 6 months to 1 year: 20 to 60 micrograms

Toddlers 1 to 3 years: 20 to 80 micrograms

Importance of chromium: Needed for normal glucose metabolism. Chromium helps to stabilize blood sugar levels.

Good sources of chromium: Red meats, whole grains grown in chromium-rich soil, and egg yolks.

Fluoride

Dietary reference intakes:

Infants 6 months to 3 years: 0.5 milligram

Toddlers 3 to 6 years: 0.7 milligram

Importance of fluoride: Actively becomes part of your baby's teeth and bones, making them stronger and the teeth more resistant to cavities (permanent teeth start forming in infancy).

Good sources of fluoride: Tea, seafood, seaweed, and some water sources. Call your local water company to determine whether your water contains fluoride. Fluoridation of municipal water supplies is a controversial issue. Health care providers have recently changed their recommendations for fluoride supplementation.

Vitamins

There are two types of vitamins: water soluble (the B complex and C) and fat soluble (A, D, E, and K). Water-soluble vitamins, which are not stored in the body, need to be replaced daily by

How Much Fluoride Is Too Much?

At the time of the writing of this book, the American Academy of Pediatrics recommends that babies under the age of six months should not be given fluoride supplements. Between six months and three years, supplement only if your child's drinking-water supply has low amounts of fluoride (less than 0.3 parts per million). Because too much fluoride can be toxic, causing a browning and crumbling of your child's teeth, do not give baby a fluoride supplement unless recommended by a physician. Most pediatricians will recommend a prescription of fluoride drops at the eight-month checkup if you are not using fluoridated water.

eating foods that contain them. Fat-soluble vitamins are stored so we can get by if they're not consumed every day.

Water-Soluble Vitamins

Six different B vitamins make up the B complex. Generally speaking, B vitamins help to release energy from food; some have additional functions.

B Complex

Recommended dietary allowances:

Infants 6 months to 1 year: Varies by individual vitamin

Toddlers 1 to 3 years: Varies by individual vitamin

Importance of B-complex vitamins: Crucial for energy and growth and to help the body process food.

Good sources of B-complex vitamins: Breast milk (if mother's intake is good), dairy products, whole grains, meats, and vegetables.

Vitamin C

Recommended dietary allowances:

Infants 6 months to 1 year: 35 milligrams

Toddlers 1 to 3 years: 40 milligrams

Importance of vitamin C: Vitamin C strengthens collagen, the material that forms the basis of all body tissues such as bone, internal organs, and so on. It makes strong bones, teeth, gums, and healthy skin. It also helps the body absorb iron, so always serve a vitamin C-rich food with iron-containing foods.

Good sources of vitamin C: Breast milk (if mother's intake is good), and fresh produce in general, especially citrus fruits, broccoli, strawberries, cantaloupe, potatoes, sweet potatoes, and tomatoes.

Fat-Soluble Vitamins

Vitamin A comes in two forms. The form in animal foods is readily used by the body. The form of vitamin A in plant foods, called beta-carotene, must be altered in the body to be used as vitamin A. Both are essential for certain functions, and beta-carotene is also an antioxidant, which protects cells from damage.

Vitamin A

Recommended dietary allowances:

Infants 6 months to 1 year: 375 micrograms

Toddlers 1 to 3 years: 400 micrograms

Importance of vitamin A: Important for growth, eyesight, strong bones, good immune function, and possibly preventing cancer.

Good sources of vitamin A: Breast milk, fortified dairy products, liver, egg yolks, yellow/orange vegetables and fruits, and dark, leafy greens.

Vitamin D

Recommended dietary allowances:

Infants 6 months to 1 year: 5 micrograms

Toddlers 1 to 3 years: 5 micrograms

Importance of vitamin D: Regulates how the body uses calcium, therefore vitamin D is essential for bone formation.

Good sources of vitamin D: Fortified milk, tuna, and fatty fish such as salmon. In addition, when sunlight hits the skin, it prompts the body to make vitamin D.

Vitamin E

Recommended dietary allowances:

Infants 6 months to 1 year: 4 milligrams

Toddlers 1 to 3 years: 6 milligrams

Importance of vitamin E: Builds healthy red blood cells and prevents the destruction of blood cells. Acts as an antioxidant, protecting cells.

Good sources of vitamin E: Breast milk, lightly processed vegetable oils, eggs, spinach, brussels sprouts, and leafy greens.

Vitamin K

Recommended dietary allowances:

Infants 6 months to 1 year: 10 micrograms

Toddlers 1 to 3 years: 15 micrograms

Importance of vitamin K: Promotes normal blood clotting.

Good sources of vitamin K: Green leafy vegetables, plus peas, green beans, cabbage, cauliflower, spinach, kelp, and liver. In addition, helpful intestinal bacteria produce vitamin K. Newborns don't have bacteria in their intestines so they are often given an injection of vitamin K at birth. This provides sufficient vitamin K until the intestinal bacteria gets established and begins making vitamin K.

Water

What does water do? Water is vital, making up about 60 percent of the body. A person can go weeks or months without food, but only a few days without water. Technically speaking, water is not a "nutrient," but it is certainly essential to survival. Water is necessary for digestion, removing body wastes, and regulating the body temperature.

The importance of water for your baby. Babies lose water daily through via evaporation from the skin, exhalation of their breath, and in urine and bowel movements. Breastfed babies get water through their mother's milk supply. So, if you are a nursing mother, it's vitally important that you drink plenty of water so you have plenty of milk with an appropriate water content.

Formula-fed babies get water from their formula, so be sure to mix it with the correct amount of water.

Offer a drink. In the beginning, babies get enough water from either breast milk or formula. Babies usually don't need additional water until four to six months of age. At this stage, you should begin offering small amounts of water several times per day. Sometimes babies may cry because they're thirsty, rather than hungry. So if it's not your older baby's typical time to eat, you might try offering water. However, if you live in a hot climate or your baby has had vomiting and/or diarrhea, then babies of all ages require additional water.

Toddler Portions— What Does It All Mean?

As your child makes the transition from baby to toddler, you need to know how much more you should be feeding your toddler. For the purposes of this book, toddler is defined as a child between one to three years old.

Figuring out your child. Your toddler's intake of formula will start to decrease as he starts drinking whole milk and eating more solids. Each baby is different as to when he is completely weaned off formula or breast milk and when he gets all his calories from solids and beverages other than formula or breast milk. As a guideline, your toddler should be taking in approximately 1,000 to 1,300 calories per day. The following lists where those calories should come from:

Summary of Nutrition Guidelines
Broken Down by Age

Nutrient	Birth to 6 months	6 to 12 months
Protein	13g	14g
Vitamins		
A (mcg)	375	375
D (mcg)	7.5	10
E (mg)	3	4
K (mcg)	5	10
C (mg)	30	35
Thiamin (mg)	0.3	0.4
Riboflavin (mg)	0.4	0.5
Niacin (mg)	5	6
B_6 (mg)	0.3	0.6
Folacin (mcg)	25	35
B_{12} (mcg)	0.3	0.5
Minerals		
Calcium (mg)	400	600
Phosphorus (mg)	300	500
Magnesium (mg)	40	60
Iron (mg)	6	10
Zinc (mg)	5	5
Iodine (mcg)	40	50
Selenium (mcg)	10	15

Calorie Distribution by Nutrients

Protein	16 grams	= 64 calories
Fat	44 grams	= 396 calories
Carbohydrate	210 grams	= 840 calories
Total		**= 1,300 calories**

Portions should be further broken down by food groups, as listed below:

Protein

Nutritionists recommend two servings or 16 grams daily. A serving equals one egg; 1 to 2 tablespoons of meat, fish, poultry; or 1 to 2 ounces of legumes, tofu, or beans.

> **Protein Foods**
> Chopped cooked egg yolk
> Shredded cheese (pressed into a ball for easy pickup)
> Cubes of soft cheese
> Baked tofu sticks
> Pureed meats with texture
> Pieces of tender, cooked flaked fish
> Peanut butter
> Scrambled egg

Fat

Remember that up to the age of two, your toddler needs a full fat diet. That's not to say that fats should overwhelm the diet—just don't serve reduced-fat foods.

Keep the fat healthy. Avoid fast food, processed foods, and snack foods that are high in unfavorable types of fat. Serve foods such as full-fat cottage cheese, yogurt, and other dairy products; peanut butter; eggs; cheese sauce on macaroni; and butter.

Reduce fat. After the age of two, gradually decrease your toddler's fat intake (for example, offer 2 percent milk) until by the age of five, she's getting no more than 30 percent of her calories from fat (for example, 1 percent or fat-free milk).

Fruits and Vegetables

Nutritionists recommend two servings daily of fruit and three servings daily of vegetables. A fruit serving for toddlers equals one quarter of a fresh fruit, sliced or cubed, or 3 ounces of juice. A vegetable serving equals 1 to 2 tablespoons of pureed vegetables.

Fruits and Vegetables
Banana slices

Ripe papaya sticks

Soft-cooked apple wedges

Orange sections with membrane removed

Avocado slices

Soft-cooked sweet potato sticks

Grains

Nutritionists recommend six servings daily. For toddlers, a serving equals one-half slice of bread, one-quarter cup cereal, or one-quarter cup rice or pasta.

Bread and Cereal

Teething biscuits

Dry unsweetened cereal without nuts or dried fruit

Bagel (hardened/dried ones make good teething rings)

Toast or bread

Graham crackers

Whole-grain crackers

Pasta

Brown rice

Mini sandwiches filled with cottage cheese

Dairy Products

Nutritionists recommend two servings daily for children aged two to six. Even for toddlers, a serving equals one cup whole milk or yogurt, or two ounces of cheese.

Start slowly, just in case. Your toddler can slowly be introduced to milk products. Yogurt is a wonderful source of protein and helpful bacteria that aid in digestion. You can continue to use breast milk or formula as an additive to your recipes.

Dairy Foods

Whole milk

Plain yogurt mixed with fruit puree

Grated cheese

Cubes of soft cheese

Cottage cheese

At Marcia's WIC clinic, the clients get monthly coupons for 100 percent juice. She's careful to teach the mothers how to use the nutrient-rich juice. She's seen too many babies and toddlers who come in with their front teeth all black and decayed from being put to bed with juice in the bottle. Its sweetness provides the right food for decay-causing bacteria in the mouth to grow and destroy teeth. Other times she sees toddlers who are in the 95th percentile or more for their weight, which means they are becoming overweight already. Upon questioning the mother, Marcia often learns that their toddler drinks anywhere from four to eight servings of juice a day. Juice is highly concentrated and rich in calories. A recent research study showed that children who drank more than 12 ounces of apple juice per day were shorter and heavier than children who drank less juice. Marcia instructs the mothers to dilute the juice half and half with water, and to serve it as a food, not as a thirst quencher!

Starting Solids

Food is the most primitive form of comfort.
—Sheilah Graham

my spooned a little mushy rice cereal into Jamie's bottle, added formula, and shook it well. The pediatrician said this would help him sleep through the night. Little Jamie was only six weeks old, and Amy and her husband were exhausted from getting up three times every night. Amy was confused, though, because she thought she wasn't supposed to give solid food until her baby was at least four months old. "Maybe this doesn't count," she rationalized, "since it's mixed with formula."

Luckily Amy mentioned the pediatrician's recommendation to her younger sister, who was studying nutrition at the local university. Her sister quickly advised her not to put cereal in the bottle, listing the potential problems and explaining that pediatricians often have so much to keep up with that they're not always aware of the latest information on food and nutrition. To her amazement, Amy found that merely stroking Jamie's back during one of his nighttime awakenings was enough to comfort him. That technique, *coupled with Jamie's getting a little older, meant that soon he woke up just once at night for a short time.*

This chapter outlines specific timeframes to introduce certain foods to your baby. There are several reasons for this.

What is the age . . . and why? Although at one time doctors advised mothers to give their babies solid food very early (ostensibly to help babies sleep through the night), pediatric experts no longer feel a baby should be introduced to solids until four to six months of age. The nervous system needs to mature so babies can recognize a spoon, coordinate swallowing, and signal when they are hungry or full. The digestive system needs to mature as well. Introducing solid foods to your baby too early may cause otherwise avoidable food allergies and may contribute to overfeeding.

How will I know? When your baby is anywhere between four and six months old, you'll start to notice these signs that she's ready for solids:

She begins to sit up well with support.

She can pick up small items.

She shows interest in food.

She begins up and down chewing movements.

She can hold her neck up and control head movements.

When to Start Solids

You should discuss with your pediatrician the proper time to introduce solids to your child. Babies generally are still on breast milk or formula before four months of age and can usually do without solids until they reach six months. Nutritionally, babies don't need solids before they're six months old; in fact, many babies cannot tolerate them any earlier.

Playing it safe. Some experts in the field suggest waiting until six months to introduce solids. Up until then, your baby would receive 100 percent of her nourishment from breast milk or formula.

Don't use cereal as a sleeping aid. Some well-meaning relatives may try to persuade you to put cereal in baby's bottle before six months of age, but hold fast. It is not a good idea. Research shows that it does not help baby sleep through the night—he'll sleep through the night when he's matured sufficiently, usually between two and four months of age. In addition, the baby's intestines are not mature enough to efficiently digest cereal.

Don't risk it. Adding food to a bottle of formula or breast milk creates a texture that may delay baby's learning of more advanced feeding skills. More important, a baby sucking food through a nipple may be at risk for choking and aspirating (breathing in) the food. There are further good reasons for delaying your baby's introduction to solids, including the potential for allergies as well as digestive and developmental reasons.

Avoiding Allergies

One reason pediatricians recommend delaying the introduction of solids until four to six months is to avoid allergies in babies.

Why do babies get allergies? A food allergy occurs when the baby's body has an abnormal reaction after eating a certain food item. This is caused by the absorption of large, only partially digested protein molecules. The body thinks these large protein molecules are foreign invaders that need to be destroyed, so it mounts an immune response.

Allergy symptoms. The immune response results in symptoms typical of food allergies, such as skin rash, digestive upset, and respiratory discomfort.

Common allergy foods. The foods most likely to cause allergic reactions include milk, wheat, corn, soy products, egg whites, citrus fruits, nuts, berries, and shellfish. As a general rule, you should wait at least until the one-year mark before introducing such foods.

Immature Digestive System

Why wait? Your baby's digestive system is not sufficiently developed to handle solid foods until around at least four months of age, when her system begins to secrete the main digestive enzyme, amylase, which breaks down starches and complex carbohydrates. This means that if your baby eats foods and starches before this time, she won't digest them; they'll pass right through her system into the diaper, possibly causing distress along the way. Too much undigested food passing through her system may damage your baby's kidneys, lead to respiratory problems, or create unnecessary food allergies.

Other Developmental Reasons

The physical challenge. During the first four months of his life, your baby's oral development changes from a simple suck to a more mature sucking pattern. Thus he swallows by sucking then using a tongue thrust motion to complete the swallow. Any solids given now will automatically be pushed out of the mouth with the tongue thrust motion.

Let it come naturally. Around four to six months of age, a baby begins to show signs of being ready, both behaviorally and developmentally, to learn new feeding skills. By now the mature suck has developed and up and down chopping/chewing motions begin. This is a good time for you to introduce your baby to solids. It exposes her to new textures and tastes and stimulates her to learn how to move things around in her mouth. The other important reason for introducing solids is to include additional nutrients to your baby's diet. For instance, a newborn has enough iron stores to last about four to six months; after that dietary iron is needed from solid foods.

Watch for signs. Babies let their parents know when they are ready for solids; they may begin to request breast milk or formula more often than before. However, at this time they continue to get most of the nutrition they need from breast milk or formula.

If all goes well. . . . If your baby is gaining weight properly and your pediatrician confirms this, you don't need to start him on solid foods before he's four to six months old. Then, when it's time, make sure he first exhibits the developmental signs mentioned previously that show he's ready for solids. If you notice that your baby is not gaining weight and seems hungry after being breastfed or bottlefed, check with your pediatrician for advice.

What Solids to Feed First

It is important to begin with foods that supplement breast milk or formula. These foods are sources of protein, iron, and carbohydrates.

Infant Cereals

The order in which you introduce new foods is important. As I mentioned before, you want to be very careful not to introduce allergenic foods too early. Many parents begin with cereal—specifically iron-fortified infant cereals.

A good choice. The American Academy of Pediatrics and doctors also recommend infant cereals. These cereals are also enriched with calcium; phosphorus; and the B vitamins thiamin, riboflavin, and niacin, which your baby needs to grow and develop. Cereals made for older children or adults are not nutritionally formulated for babies, and their texture may be unsuitable for your baby and cause her to gag.

Starting out. When introducing cereal to your baby, choose a single-grain, iron-fortified cereal. That way, if your baby is intolerant of or has difficulty digesting a particular grain, you will have no difficulty figuring out which one caused the problem. Rice-based and oat-based cereals are common first choices because they are the least likely to cause an allergic reaction. (Try to wait until your baby is a year old before introducing wheat cereal, because many babies are prone to allergic reactions to wheat.)

Making the cereal. Prepare commercial cereal by combining the recommended amount in a bowl, with breast milk, formula, or lukewarm water. (Milk or formula instead of water is preferable, as it will boost the nutrient content.) Add liquid to make the food a consistency that your baby can swallow easily. You may want to buy a jar of "1st Foods" baby food to get an idea of a good beginning consistency for baby. Start with one teaspoon of cereal mixed with milk or water per meal. As your baby gets used to the new sensation of eating, you can increase the amount.

Safety Tips

- If you use commercial baby food from a jar, listen for a whooshing, popping, or clicking noise when you open the jar. Also, feel for the center of the lid to pop up. If either fails to happen, it means that the seal has been broken, and the food may be spoiled or contaminated. Return the food to the store or discard it; do *not* give it to your baby.

- You can, if you want, heat the food by placing the opened jar in a pan of hot water (if the jar fits in a bottle steamer, try using the steamer to warm the jar). Always stir to distribute heat evenly, and before feeding your baby, test the food's temperature by putting a drop on your wrist.

- Spoon the baby's portion into a plastic bowl. If you feed directly from the jar, you transfer your baby's saliva to the remaining food; the jar in effect then acts as a bacterial petri dish, and unused portions must be discarded. Refrigerate unused portions of jarred foods, but discard any left in the bowl. Throw away unused foods within twenty-four hours.

Gradual changes. Introduce a new grain no more frequently than every three to seven days, leaving an interval of a few days in between to watch for any allergic reactions. Allergic reactions may include excessive gas, hives, diarrhea, skin rash, vomiting, runny nose, and nasal congestion. Do not give your baby mixed-grain cereals until you are certain he can tolerate the various individual grains they contain.

First Feedings

The right timing and amount. A good time for your baby's first solid food experience is halfway through a meal (breast or bottle), when hunger has been partly satisfied. For the first feeding, just give the baby a spoonful or two of a single food item.

Starting out slowly. As suggested earlier, rice or oat cereal is good for starters. Offer the cereal slowly. Keep in mind that your baby is experiencing a new sensation and needs to learn how to use her tongue to transfer the food laterally in her mouth and then swallow. The tongue thrust reflux that she's used so far could send much of the first food offered running down her chin, so be patient! This doesn't mean she doesn't like the food; she's just unfamiliar with the taste and texture of the food and is learning how to swallow differently now.

A gradual transition. Offer the same food for a week, gradually increasing the amount to about three or four tablespoons per feeding. The next week, offer another type of iron-fortified cereal. Start with one meal a day for the first two weeks, then gradually go to two meals a day.

Making the feeding pleasant. Feed your baby in a small baby chair, on your lap, or in a high chair. It is best to introduce a new food when you are feeling relaxed and unhurried, and your baby, too, is calm and happy. A tense atmosphere may turn the baby off both the food and the eating experience.

Communicating with your child. Learn your baby's body language. If your baby is hungry, he'll appear excited, waving his hands and kicking his feet when you bring him a bottle or spoon with the food you are about to give him. He'll lean forward and open his mouth. If your baby isn't hungry, he'll close his mouth and turn away or even fall asleep. No baby wants to be force-fed. Remember to help him recognize and respect his internal cues for hunger and satiety.

Don't panic. As long as your baby is healthy and growing at an average rate, you can try at a later time to feed her a food she's rejected. Try reintroducing that particular food a few days or weeks later, as her tastes may have changed. If your baby still does not want or like the new food, let it be. Everyone has food likes and dislikes, and you are learning about your baby's. If you attempt to force your baby to eat foods that she does not like, you may be setting the stage for poor eating habits and creating negative associations with food and mealtime. No food is irreplaceable. Find other nutritious foods that your child will enjoy.

It was December 7, Jamie's five-month birthday. Amy was going to feed him cereal from a spoon for the first time, as he seemed ready. After all, he was holding his head up and looking interested in what Amy and her husband, John, were eating. It was the early evening feeding and John had the camera in hand—ready to take a picture for their "Baby's First Year" album.

Amy fed Jamie about half a bottle, then propped him up on her lap with her arm supporting his head. First she showed him the clean spoon, then scooped a bit of cereal into it. Jamie looked at it and waved his little arms but didn't open his mouth. Amy opened her mouth wide and Jamie soon followed suit. Amy slipped the tip of the spoon in his mouth; he closed it around the spoon. "Success!" Amy thought—but only for an instant. The cereal came right back out, down Jamie's chin, just as John snapped the picture. "Oops," squealed Amy with delight. "Let's try that again!" Learning together, Amy and Jamie will soon have feeding time down to a fine art.

Vegetables

Once your baby has accepted cereal, you'll want to introduce finely pureed or strained vegetables rich in vitamins A and C and other important nutrients.

Getting your baby to like veggies. If you give a baby fruit before vegetables, he may not be nearly as pleased with the taste of vegetables. Follow the same steps as cereals: Introduce one new food at a time, three to seven days apart, and keep an eye out for allergic reactions. As you did with cereals, offer single foods, such as pureed peas or mashed squash, before combining foods.

Playing it safe. Check the puree carefully for any vegetable bits to make certain there are no hard chunks or pieces larger than a small pea—the puree should be very smooth in the first stages. Although introducing new textures is

> # Don't Overdo It!
>
> The introduction to chunkier foods takes time and patience. Try testing with foods your baby really likes (such as sweet potatoes). You may find that, at first, your baby holds the food in his mouth, and it seems as though he'll choke. To prevent choking, make sure the texture is not hard. Chunks should be soft, and only give him small bites.

important, babies can choke quite easily at this stage, and large, hard chunks are dangerous. Make sure the food is thoroughly cooked and mashed. Also, be sure to discard all seeds and pits. As your baby's eating abilities advance, you'll want her to try foods with a slightly thicker texture and she'll be able to handle soft chunks.

Start with a small portion on the tip of your baby spoon. Feed the baby one portion at a time, and increase the amount only gradually. Again, don't force-feed your baby. Let her set her own limits.

Some Don'ts on Vegetables

In some parts of the country, many vegetables, including root vegetables, such as beets, turnips, carrots, and collard greens, contain large amounts of nitrates, a chemical that can cause "blue baby syndrome," an unusual type of anemia (low blood count) in young infants. These nitrates originate from animal manure or chemical fertilizer and make their way into the water and soil in which vegetables grow. You may want to avoid preparing these vegetables until your baby is at least one year old.

Fruits

Pureed fruit is delicious, and babies accept it easily. It is an excellent complement to cooked cereals, vegetables, and yogurt.

Starting out slowly. As with other early foods, introduce one fruit at a time before combinations. Good early choices are applesauce, bananas, and peaches. Follow the same steps as previously described.

Some Don'ts on Fruit

• Do not offer highly acidic citrus fruits to your baby until after the first year. These fruits include oranges, grapefruit, and pineapple. They are too much work for your baby's immature digestive system and are often allergenic.

• Do not put your baby to bed with fruit juice instead of formula or breast milk. This will lead to early tooth decay because of the high sugar content. Also, juice running into their ears via the eustachian tube may cause an ear infection, just as formula and breast milk can. Juice is a concentrated food, so wait until baby is six to eight months old to serve it, and always dilute it with an equal part of water.

• Don't give your baby berries during the first year. It's hard to catch all the tiny berry seeds that may cause your baby to gag. Strawberries make a good fruit puree, but don't introduce them until after the first year.

Meat and Alternatives

Starting out slowly. The time to introduce strained meat, fish, and poultry or alternatives such as dried beans, lentils, or egg yolks is when your baby is about nine to ten months old. This is after he has become used to vegetables and fruits and is not quite so surprised when you offer new foods.

How does meat benefit baby? Meats are rich in protein, iron, and zinc. They help fulfill nutritional needs for your baby's incredibly active growth period.

When you introduce your baby to eggs, offer only the yolk for starters. Babies under a year old should not be given the egg white because it is highly allergenic in some infants. The yolk should be hard-boiled.

A gradual process. Continue to offer one new single food at a time. You might start with chicken (see the recipes in chapter 6), for example, to see how your baby adapts. Then, after a few days during which she shows no allergic reaction, try beef, and so on. When she is tolerant of a variety of foods, you can mix different kinds of food together. Keep an eye out for bones or pieces too large for a baby to handle.

Conquering the Cup

Sometime between six to nine months of age, your baby will be able to form his lips around the edge of a cup and drink—as long as you hold the cup. When you and your baby decide to make this big leap, the following tips may help to make this transition a smooth and happy experience for both of you:

Start early. About a month before you want to begin supplementing bottle feedings with a cup, introduce the cup to your child. It will be a much easier transition if your baby first understands that the cup can hold her favorite liquid, such as breast milk or formula, just as a bottle does.

Moving up to the sippy cup. Begin the transition gradually by adding a sippy cup during bottle feedings. A sippy cup is made of plastic with a tightly fitting lid that has a small spout out of which the baby can drink. You can purchase these types of cups in any baby department or at the grocery store. A good time to give your baby the cup may be when you are also going to have a drink. In this way, you can share a special "mom and baby" drink break. Make sure that you show excitement each time your baby takes his first sips from the cup. Positive reinforcement will help your baby know that he's doing something that makes you very happy, and in turn he'll feel good about himself.

Next Steps

As the baby increases her intake of solid foods, the need to breastfeed declines. Some mothers prefer to continue breastfeed-

Suggestion

Use a sippy cup with a spout. Your baby will not be able to drink successfully out of a regular, grown-up cup until well into the toddler years. Remember that manipulating and holding a cup is very different from using a bottle, so expect a lot of dropped cups until the baby is accustomed to the new drinking device. This means that you need a cup that is not only spill-proof, but also drop-proof, so it doesn't crack or break when dropped.

ing until baby can drink from a cup, thus avoiding bottles altogether. Other mothers choose to breastfeed for several years, letting the child decide when to stop. Babies who have had frequent supplemental bottles from an early age tend to wean themselves earlier than other babies.

Weaning your baby. Just as choosing to breastfeed is a very personal choice, so is weaning your baby from the breast. Once you decide to wean, contact your lactation educator or doctor for a recommendation on what to use as replacement feedings (formula or cow's milk, depending in part on the age of your child). Keep in mind that if your baby is allergic to the liquid used in replacement feedings, you may have to reconsider weaning.

Weaning safety. Don't start weaning when you or your baby are sick, if you currently have mastitis or a plugged duct, or while your baby is experiencing a growth spurt. Depending on your circumstances, you can choose to wean gradually or rapidly, both of which are described to follow.

Gradual Weaning

This is the most desirable form of weaning because it's least disruptive to both mother and baby.

The weaning steps. Start by keeping track of how many times per day your baby is nursing and how many minutes he takes to complete the meal. Each day, drop one or two minutes of your total feeding time from the usual duration of the meal. Every other day, drop an entire breast feeding and replace it with a bottle feeding or a cup feeding. Drop the feedings in order of your baby's preference, saving his favorite feeding for last—typically the one before bedtime or first thing in the morning. Over a matter of several weeks, your baby will probably be weaned with the least discomfort to the mother and the least disruption and adjustment for the baby.

Bags of frozen small vegetables come in handy to relieve breast discomfort during weaning because they can easily mold to the shape of your breast. Mark these bags as ice packs, and do not eat the peas because they will have slightly thawed and re-frozen many times.

Rapid Weaning

Though it is not recommended, rapid weaning is sometimes necessary under medical emergencies or if mother needs to take medication that may harm her milk, but it can be painful for the mother and requires baby to quickly adjust to a new routine, which may be upsetting.

Taking the proper steps. If you must use the rapid weaning method, pick a date to begin exclusively bottlefeeding your baby. Decide from that time on that you will no longer breastfeed (it is recommended by lactation consultants that you don't let your baby breastfeed during rapid weaning, since it will stimulate more milk production), and do the following:

- To help breast discomfort, wear a firm-fitting sport bra twenty-four hours a day, and apply ice or bags of frozen peas or other small vegetables to the breasts as much as possible.
- Stop eating or drinking foods with caffeine, such as sodas, chocolate, coffee, and caffeinated teas.
- Turn your back to the shower spigot so that you don't stimulate the nipples with the hot water.

Rapid weaning results. Soon, your breasts will become engorged; this will trigger your body to stop milk production. Within three to five days, your milk levels should drop significantly.

Contact your physician regarding taking over-the-counter pain medications during weaning. Again, gradual weaning is more comfortable and preferred if it's possible for you to do so.

What to do after weaning. After the child is weaned, be sure to continue to give formula if she is less than one year old. If the transition has occurred after the age of one, use whole cow's milk, not two percent or other low-fat milks. Full-fat milk is needed for proper development. Only after the age of two should you begin to gradually decrease the fat content of your child's milk. By the age of five, your child can be drinking the same one percent or nonfat milk that the rest of the family drinks.

CHAPTER 5

Preparing Homemade Baby Food

Trust yourself. You know more than you think you do.
—Dr. Benjamin Spock

Sunday afternoon was Vicki's special time to prepare much of her family's food for the week. She was a master at this—and it made the week's meals go so smoothly! Her two older boys ran through the kitchen, with neighbor kids trailing, grabbing handfuls of baby carrots on the way. "Hey," she scolded good-naturedly, "I was just getting ready to cook those for Steven!"

Steven—cooing away in his high chair, arms and legs waving madly—didn't seem to mind. She gave him a kiss on her way to the refrigerator for more carrots. She had one pan of boiling water with a steamer basket, and five different vegetables and four different fruits—all washed and ready to steam, one at a time. The food processor was on the counter, ready to do its part. Vicki would be done in no time, and was confident that she was feeding her family healthful food.

You don't need to be a gourmet chef to make baby food, but you will get a feeling of satisfaction from making your baby's food yourself! You can prepare many of these recipes by following the guidelines in this chapter. You'll also learn how to save time by preparing homemade foods in large quantities, then freezing them in small portions for later use. This chapter explains how to safely make, freeze, store, thaw, and reheat the foods you prepare.

The Safety Factor

Because of their immature immune systems, babies are extremely vulnerable to bacteria that may contaminate food. It is imperative that you take the proper steps to ensure that you are preparing your baby's food safely. Let's learn about how food becomes unsafe and what you can do to prevent contamination.

How Food Becomes Unsafe

Contamination in this case refers to the unintended presence of microorganisms in food. There are three types of hazards to watch out for.

1. *Biological hazards:* Bacteria, viruses, parasites, and fungi. Raw animal foods such as meat, eggs, and milk may contain some of these harmful organisms. Fruits and vegetables, if not washed thoroughly, can also contain disease-causing microorganisms. Poor food-handling practices, such as not washing hands and kitchen surfaces, can transfer harmful bacteria to foods. Contamination by bacteria is the greatest threat to food safety.

2. *Chemical hazards:* Pesticides, food additives, and preservatives, as well as cleaning supplies and toxic materials. Pesticide residues may remain on produce from the field, while processed foods may contain artificial additives and preservatives. Cleaning supplies that leak, spill, or are not adequately rinsed off can also be a source of contamination. Certain cooking methods, such as high heat (broiling or grilling foods that contain animal fat) can cause the formation of toxic compounds that cause cancer.

3. *Physical hazards:* Foreign matter, such as dirt. This gets into the food via unwashed foods, dirty hands, and unclean kitchen equipment.

General Food Safety Tips

As you prepare baby food, follow these food safety procedures. They are basic to keeping food safe, so don't miss any steps.

Wash your hands frequently. Keeping your hands clean and free from bacteria when preparing food and caring for baby is important. Use warm water to moisten hands. Apply liquid soap, rub hands together for a full twenty seconds, being careful to get under and around nails, rinse thoroughly, and dry with a clean towel. Avoid antibacterial soaps, as they are not necessary. They don't get rid of any more bacteria than proper handwashing does, but they may contribute to the problem of bacteria that are resistant to antibiotics.

Wash your cooking utensils immediately after use. Wash all your dishes, silverware, pans, cooking utensils, cutting boards, and kitchen knives with hot water and soap, then apply a sanitizing solution to the cutting boards and kitchen knives to prevent cross contamination—that is bacteria from one food getting onto another food. Spray the sanitizing solution on, let it set two minutes, then rinse thoroughly. Use this solution throughout your kitchen—on counters and faucets, too, before starting to prepare food. Air-drying is the recommended method of drying to avoid recontamination from a potentially dirty dish towel and further handling.

Keep perishable foods cold. Perishable foods include meats, eggs, dairy products, and recently cooked foods. These foods should not be left out at room temperature for more than two hours. Bacteria grows rapidly at room temperature and can quickly reach levels that can cause illness. Some sources believe that up to four hours at room temperature is acceptable, but most professional organizations recommend only two hours. Especially where baby is concerned, two hours is

To make a safe and economical sanitizing solution, mix 1 teaspoon of household bleach with 2 cups of water. Store in a spray bottle and make a fresh batch weekly. This solution is strong enough to kill microorganisms, but weak enough to not bleach fabric. Keep out of the reach of children.

probably the safest recommendation to follow. Check the temperature of your refrigerator; it should be between 35 and 38 degrees Fahrenheit—never above 40 degrees Fahrenheit. You should chill leftover foods in shallow containers, and definitely before two hours have passed.

Cook foods thoroughly. Make sure that internal temperatures get high enough to kill microbes (use a meat thermometer). When reheating food, bring it to a temperature that will kill bacteria, 165 degrees Fahrenheit or greater. Then let it cool before serving to baby.

For more food safety tips, visit the Web site for "Fight Bac!", a national food safety campaign to fight bacteria (www.fight bac.org).

Clean Versus Sanitary or Sterilized

Clean means free of visible dirt. Sanitary means free of harmful microorganisms.

Don't let looks fool you. Clean-looking food, equipment, and utensils may not be sanitary. If you sanitize equipment (not food) with the spray described before, you'll kill bacteria and microorganisms. If you sterilize an item, you expose it to high heat (usually by boiling it), which effectively kills most bacteria.

Cook it clean. Cooking food will take care of killing bacteria, too. Washing will generally remove all dirt, but not necessarily chemicals such as pesticide residues that may be trapped under the wax used to keep produce from drying out.

Scrubbing and/or peeling fresh produce is your best assurance of removing all possible contaminates.

Kitchen Equipment

Take a quick inventory of your kitchen equipment to see whether you have the equipment you will need to make homemade baby food. You probably already have most of these items; if not, consider putting them on your baby shower list!

Here's a list of suggested items and notes on their use.

Food Processors or Blenders

You'll need either a food processor (a unit with a large plastic container on top of it that contains a blade) or a common kitchen blender.

Making the choice. Both the food processor and the blender will make baby food, but the food processor is typically easier and requires less use of added water because the food is processed easily in the large container rather than in the narrow blender.

Other options. Another suggestion for a purchase is a commercial-grade blender. I burned up the motors on two regular blenders by mixing basic recipes such as peas and potatoes without adding much water. VitaMix is an example of a good commercial-grade blender. Most blenders that will make juice from fresh produce, such as the VitaMix, are powerful enough to work.

- *Handheld mixer.* This is easy to clean and used for pureeing single servings.
- *Moulis.* This manual grinder (the name comes from the French word for grind) is handy for grinding food and removing skins.
- *Wire mesh strainer.* If you cannot afford a food processor or blender, or live in an area with frequent power outages that would prevent you from using electrical appliances, you can make baby food with a strainer. Just cook the food thoroughly, then force it through the strainer using the back of a spoon. Get a medium gauge strainer for proper consistency. The gauge refers to the amount of space there is between the wires that form the mesh. A fine gauge will not let enough food pass through, and a large gauge will not make the food smooth enough.

Other Kitchen Items

• *Two cutting boards.* (Plastic is recommended because it can be easily sanitized between uses.) Use one for meats, fish, and poultry. Use the second cutting board for fruits and vegetables.

• *French or chef's knife for chopping*
• *Paring knife for paring fruits and vegetables*
• *Measuring spoons for measuring out ingredients*
• *Liquid measuring cups for measuring liquid ingredients*
• *Dry measuring cups for measuring dry ingredients*
• *Cooking spoons for mixing*
• *Rubber spatula for scooping out purees into containers*
• *Can opener*
• *Mixing bowls*
• *Steamer basket.* Collapsible stainless steel type so it fits in any size saucepan or bamboo basket.

• *Thermometers.* Meat thermometer, oven thermometer, refrigerator/freezer thermometer

• *Small and large saucepans and medium skillet with lids.* Do not use any old cookware in which the aluminum comes into contact with the food. Aluminum is good at conducting heat evenly, but should be covered with other surfaces so it does not come into contact with food.

• *Glass dish with lid.* Use this for microwave cooking, if you have a microwave.

Sterilizing Equipment

Sterilizing options. Simply boiling feeding equipment in a pot of water for ten minutes will sterilize it. A dishwasher can sterilize, too, if it has a cycle that heats the water higher than what comes from the hot water heater—140 degrees Fahrenheit or more. Check your owner's manual. Additionally, using a dishwasher detergent that has chlorine in it will also sanitize. Wash your feeding equipment with similar items, such as all bottles and nipples together. Don't, for example, put a casserole dish in your dishwasher when you're cleaning your baby's items. Oils from such dishes are swooshed around during the washing cycle, and can become trapped in bottles and nipples, from which they're not easily rinsed.

Cooking Methods

It's important that you match the most appropriate cooking method—baking, boiling, steaming, and microwaving—with the food you are preparing. You'll be cooking items until tender, using one of the basic methods described below.

Baking

Baking is ideal for foods that are hard and starchy, such as sweet potatoes (or potatoes in general), as well as for squash, apples, and meats.

The health benefits of baking. Baking is not only easy, but it retains many of the nutrients in foods. The heat from baking may destroy some of the vitamins, but the minerals will remain intact.

General baking guidelines. For the most part, you'll use a baking temperature of 350 degrees Fahrenheit, baking items around 45 minutes to one hour, which is longer than other cooking methods. Be sure to use your oven's middle rack to ensure that foods bake evenly. Specific instructions are given in the recipes that follow. Cover your food to avoid spillage or contact with other foods in your oven. Stick-free baking pans work best.

Boiling

Not the healthiest route. Boiling is easy, but you can lose almost 50 percent of the nutrients during the cooking process. With most boiled items, therefore, you will want to cover the pot to preserve nutrients and try to use the cooking water, which will have nutrients in it. Boiling takes 8 to 10 minutes for most vegetables. Check tenderness by piercing with a fork.

What to boil? Boiling is ideal for foods such as chicken and beef. Boil items until tender and make sure no pink remains in meats. I boiled chicken when first introducing it to my baby, simply because I wanted to be absolutely sure that it was free from bacteria, such as salmonella.

Steaming

Keeping it healthy. This is an especially good way to cook vegetables and fruits, since it retains more nutrients than boiling. Because food doesn't actually come into contact with boiling water during the steaming process, nutrients are not leached out into the water and lost. The heat itself, though, does destroy some of the vitamins, so steam as lightly as possible.

Steaming Options
Collapsible steamer. You can use a collapsible stainless steel steamer basket, which goes into a saucepan or large pot with enough water in the bottom to come up to the bottom of the steamer. Steam just until tender—the fruit or vegetable is pierced

easily with a fork or sharp knife tip. If steaming tough items, such as hard winter squash, check the water level occasionally to make sure it doesn't all boil away; add more water if necessary.

Bamboo steamer. You can also use a bamboo steamer as found in Asian markets. This type of steamer must be approximately the same diameter as the pot you are putting it over—it sits on top of your pot and has its own lid. Put one or two inches of water in your pan, bring to a boil, then place the basket with food in it and the lid on, on top of the pot with boiling water. Again, steam until tender. Most things steam quickly. For instance, broccoli pieces take only about three to four minutes to become tender.

Steamer basket. You'll find the steamer basket in most grocery stores. As a general rule of thumb, you should place the basket in a larger pot and fill the pot with enough water to barely touch the bottom of the steamer basket. Most foods steam in 5 to 10 minutes.

Microwaving

This is another option to consider for convenience.

Microwaving benefits. Microwaving provides fast cooking—especially for fruits, vegetables, and hot cereals—with a minimal nutrient loss. The larger the item, the more time you'll save. For instance, it takes about as long to steam broccoli florets as it does to microwave them, but potatoes can be "baked" in about ten minutes versus 40 to 60 minutes in a traditional oven.

Microwaving precautions. Never heat or cook with plastic in the microwave, and do not let plastic wrap come into contact with food in the microwave. Heating plastic causes toxic chemicals from the plastic to leach into the food. New, long-term research is underway, but some researchers feel that a lifetime exposure to some of these chemicals will cause cancer or other chronic disorders. To be safe, use a glass dish with a glass lid when cooking in the microwave.

Caution: Beware of hot spots, or regional pockets of heat, which may cause severe burning. Stir foods midway through and after the cooking process. Let foods sit several minutes after you remove them from the microwave, as heat continues to build for a short time. Remember to use the microwave only to prepare baby food that you will cool and store. Do not use the microwave to cook or heat baby's food because of the risk of hot pockets.

Cooling After Cooking

After cooking baby food, you need to cool it properly to avoid contamination.

Cool from safety hazards. The danger zone at which bacteria grows best is between 40 degrees and 140 degrees Fahrenheit. Therefore, it's important to avoid leaving food in this temperature range for any length of time.

Cooling method. When cooling baby food, begin by taking the food from the pan it was cooked in and dividing it into smaller portions into shallow containers; then place the containers into an ice-water bath. Leave the filled containers in an ice bath to cool for fifteen to twenty minutes before placing them into your refrigerator or freezer. This will prevent unnecessary bacteria growth that would result from heat, and will also allow the food to cool without changing the internal temperature of your refrigerator or freezer.

Quick cooling. If you're in a hurry, it is safe to put the foods into shallow containers (less than two inches deep) and put

General Tips for Making Your Own Baby Food

- Choose bland, easily digestible foods, such as boiled carrots, mashed potatoes, green peas, or applesauce.
- Wash your hands carefully, and clean all utensils thoroughly before preparing food.
- Peel and wash all fresh produce.
- Using the cooking techniques given earlier in this chapter, cook the solids first (unless you're working with bananas). Nearly all foods should be cooked before giving to baby so that they can be adequately pureed. (As baby gets older, fruits and vegetables don't need to be cooked as much because he is able to tolerate rougher textures.)
- Blend the cooked solids well in a food processor, blender, or food mill until the mixture becomes semi-liquid in consistency.
- Do not add salt or sugar for reasons mentioned in previous chapters.
- Select fresh foods over frozen when possible, and stay away from canned products, which may be high in salt or sugar.
- Stay away from strong spices, such as pepper or garlic, which your baby may find unpleasant to eat. Don't assume that making baby food means it has to be bland. Your baby will enjoy the hearty taste of pure foods.
- Add certain hypoallergenic natural herbs for seasoning if you feel it's necessary.
- Keep homemade baby food frozen or refrigerated until use.
- Avoid canning baby food due to the risk of botulism. It is much safer to freeze baby food for long-term storage.

immediately into the refrigerator—it won't hurt today's modern refrigerators.

After cooling. Once cooled, if you're not going to use the food within three days, freeze it. Of course, you may want to serve baby some of the food right away, in which case just let it come to a reasonable temperature that you test before serving. Spreading it out will help it cool more quickly.

Blending Purees

Because blending is the method that you will use most during your baby's early life, let's spend some time understanding the best way to blend purees.

- Cook item(s) until tender, using one of the basic methods described.
- Let items cool slightly so you can handle the food without burning yourself.
- Cut the item(s) that you want to puree into small pieces (usually no larger than one-inch squares). *Note:* It's a good idea to cook foods in larger pieces to minimize cut surface area. The less surface area exposed to the heat of cooking, the fewer nutrients will be lost.
- Always save some of the liquid you cooked with in case you need to thin your mixture—or you can add breast milk or formula if additional liquid is needed.
- Process these small portions in a blender or food processor until their texture is smooth, adding liquid as needed. (Remember, if you don't have either of these appliances, just mash the cooked food through a medium gauge strainer with the back of a spoon.)

- Again, add liquid if necessary to attain the consistency appropriate for your baby's developmental stage.

Freezing

If you are a working parent who needs to cook ahead of time, or you prefer cooking in large quantities to save time, then freezing will work well for you.

Saving money with freezing. The freezing method is economical because you can buy foods on sale, prepare them, and store until you need them.

Freezing preparation. Designate some space in your freezer specifically for your baby's food. Be careful not to pack your freezer tightly; the fan must be able to circulate cold air around all items. Keep your freezer at 0 degrees Fahrenheit.

Better safe than sorry. If power should go out, keep the freezer door closed as much as possible. If meats, perishables, or dishes you've prepared that contain meats or other perishables thaw, you must use immediately or throw away. If the temperature of the food climbs above 40 degrees Fahrenheit for two hours or more, throw the food out. (Use your meat thermometer here!) If fruits and vegetables thaw slightly, they can be refrozen without food safety concerns, but quality will suffer, as the refreezing will break down

Suggestion

Buy a jar of baby food early on just to see the texture that you will want to achieve. Baby food manufacturers know what textures infants enjoy and can handle at various stages.

the cell structure and make additional ice crystals, leaving the food mushy and wetter than normal.

Guidelines for Freezing

1. Decide which containers you want to use for freezing. (You can seal food in moisture-proof wrappings, such as wax paper, foil, plastic containers, or resealable plastic bags. Some people also use the ice cube method, in which you fill an ice cube tray with small cube-sized servings and seal it with plastic wrap.)

2. Once frozen, remove the food cubes and store in containers or resealable plastic bags. Thaw just as many portions as you need for your baby's feedings. (See instructions on thawing near the end of this chapter.)

3. Put food into the freezer only after it has cooled down (see previous directions). Putting hot food into the freezer raises the freezer temperature, possibly thawing food that's already frozen.

4. After food has cooled to 40 degrees or less, measure out portions appropriate for your baby and place in your plastic containers, ice cube trays, or resealable plastic bags.

Seal the bags carefully and label with the name of the food or recipe, the date you prepared it, and the storage life (two months, for example; see table "Freezer Shelf Life").

Freezing certain foods. Some foods do not freeze well because their color or texture changes. These include:

Pureed bananas (which turn brown or black)

Hard-boiled eggs (the whites become rubbery) or egg-based sauces, frostings, or meringue (texture is unappealing when

If you're a busy parent, then cooking in batches and freezing ahead of time may be the most efficient way to prepare several weeks' worth of meals. Keep in mind that you should never refreeze food that has been thawed. Refrigerate leftovers promptly in clean containers, and throw out unused food after twenty-four hours. Making enough meals for a three-day feeding schedule has worked for me. If you're going to use the food within three days, it is not necessary to freeze it. The chart on page 80 provides a list of basic foods and general freezing times for each.

thawed). Raw eggs can be frozen successfully by taking out of the shell and putting into a jar. Be sure to wash hands and utensils, countertops, and anything else that came in contact after handling raw eggs. After thawing, cook the eggs thoroughly before eating to avoid the risk of salmonella.

Tofu (freezing changes the texture to be firmer and sponge-like—desirable at times, but not easy for baby to swallow)

Soft cheeses, cream cheese, cream fillings, and custards (texture is unappealing when thawed)

Avocado (turns dark—adding lemon juice can minimize this)

Fried or breaded food (becomes mushy)

Gelatin-based foods (loses consistency)

Salad greens, radishes, cucumbers, celery, raw tomatoes, scallions, eggplant, cooked potatoes, and melon (because water content is high, these produce items become mushy; thawed product texture is not acceptable)

There are no food safety issues associated with freezing any of the aforementioned foods as long as they have been handled properly before freezing.

Freezer Shelf Life

Food	Time
Breast milk	1 year
Vegetable purees	4 months
Fruit purees	4 months
Purees with milk	2 months
Purees with meat	4 months

Leaving Frozen Food for the Caregiver

Guidelines for simplicity. If you're leaving frozen food for your caregiver to feed your baby, remove enough from the freezer ahead of time so that it can thaw in the refrigerator (see directions on thawing below). If you are using the ice cube method, thaw only what you expect your baby to eat. Generally speaking, for a four- to six-month-old, six cubes of food is six ounces or approximately two feedings over six hours. Leave your caregiver detailed instructions on what to put the food in to heat it. Remember not to use the microwave to heat baby's food.

Thawing Food Safely

You can thaw frozen foods in the refrigerator but it requires planning ahead. Leave space around the food so air can circulate. You can also thaw food under cold running water for no longer than two hours. Never thaw foods at room temperature or with hot water. Doing so allows bacteria to multiply on the warm surface of the food while the interior remains frozen. Use a microwave oven for thawing only when you plan to cook the food immediately or if you continue to finish cooking in the microwave. Remember to check carefully for hot spots before serving the food to your baby.

Warming for Feeding

Always heat baby foods with warm water or on the stovetop. If you're using the microwave to warm foods, be aware of the heating precautions mentioned earlier. Make sure your caregiver knows how to warm baby's food.

Warming safely. Always test the temperature of the food by touching it to your wrist or upper lip (and instruct your caregiver to do so). If it's too hot for you, then it's way too hot for the baby. Remember to discard any food that has come into contact with the feeding utensil because baby's saliva will have contaminated it. Reheat food only once; after that, it should be thrown away.

You may be tempted to open a can of applesauce or canned vegetables and mash them up thinking you have made "fresh" food. This defeats the purpose of making baby food. Canned foods or canned fruits have additives, particularly sodium and/or sugar, which baby doesn't need. (Frozen vegetables and jarred applesauce without sugar are fine.)

Pat had breastfed Christie for eighteen months. Her daughter was eating plenty of solid foods and now Pat felt the need for a little more independence and wanted her own body back. Her neighbor, though, had nursed her boys until they were two or three years old. Pat loved her baby, too, but felt there was no way she could do that. Even though she was breastfeeding just twice a day, it was getting on her nerves. Her daughter had received all the goodness of breast milk and was drinking well from a cup so she thought weaning shouldn't be difficult.

To avoid developing resentment toward her daughter, she decided to go ahead and wean Christie at eighteen months. As they went through the process, Pat still spent special time with her daughter each morning and evening; it just didn't involve nursing. Pat soon felt much better, and more in control of her life and her body again. And happy moms do make happy babies!

CHAPTER 6

The Best Food for Babies: Beginner Recipes

Bloom where you're planted.
—Mary Engelbreit

During his first four months, your baby should only have mother's milk, formula, or a combination of the two. Breast milk (of a well-nourished mother) and formula usually provide all the nutrients your baby needs from birth to four months.

Switching to solids. Sometime between four to six months, most babies are introduced to solid foods. The food you offer now must be right for both the baby's nutritional needs and level of development. You should offer the foods that contain the nutrients your baby needs with the consistency and texture that will help his eating skills.

Getting the iron intake for baby. An iron-fortified rice cereal, which has a consistency that you can change as baby's eating skills develop, is a good choice for a first food. By four to six months, the iron stores in your baby's body are depleted, and an outside source is necessary. At this age, babies will gradually be drinking

Best Foods for Baby

Babies should start solids with iron-fortified rice cereal and other non-wheat grains, pureed vegetables and fruits that are rich in vitamins A and C, and eventually meats and dairy products such as yogurt. Offer vitamin A (beta-carotene)–rich dark green or deep orange vegetables, such as pureed carrots or winter squash, plus vitamin C–rich fruit puree such as applesauce. Mashed ripe avocado is also an excellent early baby food. Avocados provide a very good source of healthful unsaturated fatty acids.

less breast milk or formula as their solid intake increases, and they will need a source of iron in their diets. Establishing a baby on an iron-fortified cereal early on in her introduction to solids will help secure her iron throughout infancy and into the toddler stage, when iron is most critical. Rice cereal mixed with breast milk or formula also provides a good balance of calories among protein, carbohydrates, and fat. Start with rice cereal, as it is the grain least likely to cause an allergic reaction.

The overall best. The best foods for babies are whole, unprocessed foods. The general categories are grain foods, vegetables, fruits, and diluted juices; meats, poultry, fish, and legumes; and whole dairy products. Of course, breast milk or formula gives way to milk and dairy products as baby gets older. The following lists show some of the best choices within those categories. As you read the lists, keep in mind that to avoid allergic reactions, some foods should not be introduced until after one year of age, as previously discussed.

Grain and cereals: Rice, barley, millet, oatmeal

Vegetables: Yellow or winter squash, yams, carrots, potatoes, asparagus, green leafy vegetables

Fruits: Applesauce, oranges, bananas, pears, peaches, prunes, tangerines, cantaloupes, honeydew melons

Juices: Apple, apricot, orange, grapefruit, pear, white grape, and low-sodium vegetable blends (Juices are concentrated foods, so throughout childhood they should be diluted with water most of the times you serve them. Dilute 1:1—half juice and half water.)

Meats and poultry: Plain, unsalted beef and chicken broth; chicken and turkey; organ meats such as beef or pork liver; lamb

Parents often ask this question: When do I start feeding my baby solid foods?

Experts recommend some time between four and six months.

Legumes: Split peas; lentils; kidney, black, lima, and navy beans; soybeans; tofu (Split peas and lentils are easiest to digest. Kidney and soybeans are the most difficult.)

Fish: Whitefish, bass, salmon, herring, sole, haddock, tuna

Milk and milk products: Milk, cottage cheese, cheese, yogurt

Keeping your baby's nutritional needs in mind, as well as his physical development at various stages, this chapter provides recipes for foods that are easy to make and that your baby will thrive on and enjoy. Most importantly, after you make a few of these recipes, you will realize how simple it is to make your own baby food.

Boiling or steaming? Many of the recipes call for boiling or steaming baby's food. Keep in mind that steaming is the preferred method for vegetables and fruits as this method preserves more nutrients than boiling. Boiling meats is a good idea though, to make sure they are thoroughly done and therefore limiting the risk of food-borne illness. Refer to chapter 4 for instructions on steaming.

Whip it up. The instructions for many of these recipes have you make a puree. Keep in mind that you can use whatever equipment you have (blender, food processor, baby food grinder, or wire mesh strainer), as long as you get the desired texture, regardless of which piece of equipment is mentioned in the recipe. It's easy to achieve a puree in a food processor without adding extra liquid. When using a blender, though, you often have to add liquid to get the blades working optimally. The amount of liquid needed is often so small that this is not usually a problem, but if you find you're using large amounts of water, then nutrients become diluted and a food processor might make food that is more nutrient-dense.

First Foods

Let's get started—your baby is old enough, hungry, and ready to eat! The foods in this section will provide needed nutrients while giving your baby a whole new world of tastes and textures to explore.

Grains

Grains form the base of the Food Guide Pyramid, which means this is the type of food people should eat the most of—and indeed they do. Grains provide 60 to 80 percent of every culture's food, around the world.

Rice Cereal

Primary nutrients: B vitamins

You'll find rice cereal in the baby food aisle of your grocery store. In a saucepan, bring the liquid to a boil. Immediately sprinkle in rice cereal while stirring constantly. Reduce heat, simmer 10 minutes until soft and water is absorbed.

Option for older babies: Rice cereal is particularly good when you add pureed fruit—try this after baby has successfully eaten fruits.

1 cup breast milk, water, or
  formula mixture
1/4 cup iron-fortified ground rice
  cereal

Barley Cereal

Primary nutrients: B vitamins

You'll find barley cereal in the baby food aisle of your grocery store. In a saucepan, bring the liquid to a boil. Immediately sprinkle in barley while stirring constantly. Simmer 10 minutes.

Options for older babies: After your baby is eating meats and therefore getting iron from other sources, you may wish to buy plain barley from the bulk food section of a natural-food store. Pulverize in a blender until coarse. Cook as above.

Barley cereal is particularly good when you add pureed fruit—try this after baby has successfully eaten fruits.

1 cup breast milk, water, or
  formula mixture
1/4 cup iron-fortified barley
  cereal

Oatmeal

Primary nutrients: Potassium and soluble fiber

¾ cup water
¼ cup iron-fortified oatmeal
  cereal

You'll find oatmeal cereal in the baby food aisle of your grocery store. In a saucepan, bring water to a boil. Sprinkle in oats while stirring constantly. Simmer 5 minutes. Serve with warm breast milk or formula.

Options for older babies: After your baby is eating meats and therefore getting iron from other sources, you may wish to buy rolled oats from the bulk food section of a natural-food store. Pulverize in a blender until coarse. Cook as above.

Oatmeal is particularly good when you add pureed fruit—try this after baby has successfully eaten fruits.

Grain Combinations
As you rule out possible allergies to grains and fruits, begin to mix them for new taste treats baby will love.

Millet-Fruit Cereal

Primary nutrients: B vitamins

You can usually find millet in the bulk bins of a natural-food store. In a saucepan, bring liquid to a boil. Immediately sprinkle in millet while stirring constantly. Simmer 10 minutes until soft and water is absorbed. Add fruit puree and stir.

1 cup breast milk, water, or
   formula
3 tablespoons ground millet
1 tablespoon favorite fruit puree

Peaches and White Rice

Primary nutrient: Vitamin C

Add rice to one cup boiling water; reduce heat, stir briefly, cover. Cook until rice is soft and water is absorbed. Place peach halves in a steamer basket in boiling water (enough water to touch the bottom of the steamer basket). Cover tightly. Cook 2 to 4 minutes. Strain. Blend in food processor to puree.

½ cup short-grain white rice
1 cup water
2 medium peaches, washed,
   peeled, pitted, and halved

Brown Versus White Rice

In the "Intermediates" section you'll see recipes that call for brown rice. You can start to feed a baby brown rice at eight months. Brown rice is nutritionally superior to white rice. Since it is not stripped of its outer hull of bran, it is richer in fiber, vitamins, and minerals. Since brown rice has three times the fiber as white rice, whenever possible, serve brown rice or even a mixture of brown and white rice once baby is old enough to digest the added fiber (about eight months old).

Rice Pudding

Primary nutrients: B vitamins, calcium, vitamin A, protein

2 cups breast milk or formula
   (after age one, use milk)
1 egg yolk
¼ teaspoon vanilla extract
1 teaspoon molasses
½ cup white rice

Combine milk, egg yolk, vanilla, and molasses in saucepan. Rinse rice, drain, and mix with other ingredients. Bring to boil, then simmer one hour. Cool. Process through blender.

Bananas and Tapioca

Primary nutrients: Potassium, calcium

Bring water to a boil in a saucepan. Gradually add tapioca, stirring constantly. Reduce heat to low and cook 5 minutes, continuing to stir constantly. Separately puree the banana and add to the mixture. Blend tapioca with yogurt and banana.

½ cup water

⅓ cup quick-cooking tapioca

1 banana

½ cup vanilla yogurt

The Musical Fruit?

Beans can give your baby gas, so start with the more easily digested legumes, such as lentils and split peas. As you introduce other beans, be sure to either soak them overnight or bring to a boil, pour off the water, then cover with fresh water and continue to cook. These methods will help to get rid of the unusual starch that is hard to digest and thus causes gas. Good news when you're in a hurry—lentils and split peas do *not* need soaking!

Thick Lentil or Split Pea "Soup"

Primary nutrients: Iron, zinc, B vitamins—especially folate, fiber

2½ cups water

1 cup lentils or split peas, rinsed

Bring water to a boil. Add rinsed lentils or split peas. Cook until tender—about 30 minutes for lentils or 45 minutes for split peas. While cooking, add more water, if necessary, depending on whether you want the puree to resemble soup or puree. Cool slightly. Pour into blender and puree.

Chickpea (Garbanzo Bean) Puree

Primary nutrients: Vitamin A, potassium, fiber

1 cup dried chickpeas

4 cups water

Presoak or boil chickpeas. Boil in water 1½ hours or until tender. Strain. Blend in food processor until smooth.

Soybean Puree

Primary nutrients: Iron, potassium, vitamin E, fiber

1 cup dried soybeans

4 cups water

Presoak or boil soybeans. Boil soybeans in water for 2½ to 3 hours or until tender. Strain. Blend in food processor until smooth.

Baby Lima Beans and Leeks

Primary nutrients: Iron, fiber

Presoak or boil lima beans. Simmer in 6 cups of water for 1½ to 2 hours or until beans are tender. Strain. Cut green ends of leeks off and prepare the white part by slicing lengthwise through most layers. Open inner layers of leek and wash thoroughly to remove all sand. In a separate pan, boil leeks in small amount of water 15 to 20 minutes, then drain. Add beans to leeks in blender and puree.

2 cups dried baby lima beans
6 cups water, plus water for boiling
3 stalks of leeks (white part only)

Vegetables and Fruits: Popular Single-Item Purees

The introduction. As a general rule (and for ease of memory), introduce yellow-colored fruits and vegetables first, orange second, and green last. Introduce a variety of vegetables before you start on the fruits, otherwise baby might refuse the vegetables in favor of the sweeter fruits. Corn and citrus fruits are an exception; you should not introduce these until your baby is one year old.

One at a time. This section is a quick reference for purees you'll make most frequently. These recipes contain just one item so they're great to use as you introduce new foods to your baby.

Pace yourself. Remember to introduce just one new food about every five days so you can determine which food caused a problem if symptoms develop. Many of these use small amounts— just double or triple if you want larger amounts that will last longer. Freeze all purees you won't use up within three days.

Vegetable Purees

Introduce a variety of vegetables before you start on the fruits, otherwise baby might refuse the vegetables in favor of the sweeter fruits. Corn and citrus fruits are an exception; you should not introduce these until your baby is one year old.

Sweet Potatoes or Yams

Primary nutrients: Beta-carotene, potassium

1 large sweet potato or yam

Preheat oven to 350 degrees F. Bake the potato for 1 hour on a foil-lined pan. Peel off the skin, chop potato or yam into cubes, and blend to a puree. Add 1 tablespoon water as needed.

Sweet Potato or Yam?

Pureed sweet potato is an excellent first baby food. It is a great source of beta-carotene, potassium, calcium, phosphorus, thiamin, and iron. Have you ever wondered what the difference is between sweet potatoes and yams? Basically, you can find two types of sweet potatoes in your local grocer: Moist-fleshed sweet potatoes have a bright orange flesh that is sweet when cooked. Dry-fleshed sweet potatoes have an ivory-colored flesh that is dry when cooked and less sweet. The moist-fleshed potato is known as a yam.

Avocado

Although technically a fruit, the avocado's lack of sweetness lends itself to being served as a vegetable.

Primary nutrients: Unsaturated fats, potassium, magnesium, vitamin E, and B vitamins

Mash the avocado with a fork, or press the avocado through a baby food grinder or wire-mesh strainer. You can add breast milk or formula to make a smoother consistency.

2 to 3 tablespoons ripe avocado, peeled

Winter Squash Puree

Primary nutrient: Beta-carotene

Preheat oven to 350 degrees F. Place squash cut-side down, on a foil-lined cookie sheet. Bake 45 minutes to one hour, until tender when pierced with a sharp knife. Cut squash to cool. Peel or scoop out of skin. Cut squash into small pieces. Puree in food processor or blender, adding water if necessary to reach desired consistency.

1 medium acorn squash (or other winter squash), cut in half

Carrots

Primary nutrient: Beta-carotene

1-pound bag of baby peeled carrots (try to buy organic)

Place carrots in a steamer basket with boiling water (enough water to touch the bottom of the steamer basket). Cover tightly. Cook 10 to 14 minutes until tender. Strain the carrots through a baby food grinder to a puree. Add a tablespoon of cooking water as needed. Be sure to read up on nitrate concerns in chapter 4.

Eggplant

Primary nutrient: Potassium

1 medium eggplant, peeled

Wash eggplant and remove seeds. Put into 1 inch of boiling water. Simmer, covered. Drain. Puree in food processor.

Broccoli Puree

Primary nutrients: Potassium, beta-carotene, vitamin C

3 sprigs broccoli

Wash sprigs. Boil or steam for 5 to 10 minutes. Drain. Mash with fork or blend in food processor until smooth; add cooking water if necessary for consistency.

Carrot Puree

Primary nutrient: Beta-carotene

Boil or steam about 10 minutes until tender. Drain. Mash with fork or puree in blender until smooth; add cooking water if necessary for consistency.

1 medium carrot, washed, peeled, sliced into 1-inch pieces

Cauliflower Puree

Primary nutrient: Potassium

Boil or steam until tender, about 10 to 15 minutes. Drain. Mash with fork or blend in food processor until smooth; add cooking water if necessary for consistency.

3 sprigs of cauliflower, washed

Celery Puree

Primary nutrient: Potassium

3 stalks of celery, washed, peeled, with leaves cut off	Chop into chunks. Boil or steam until tender, about 5 to 10 minutes. Drain. Mash with fork or blend in food processor until smooth; add cooking water if necessary for consistency

Cucumber Puree

Primary nutrient: Water

1 small cucumber, washed, peeled, and cut into 1-inch slices	Mash with fork or blend in food processor until smooth. Cucumber does not need to be cooked.

Lentil Puree

Primary nutrients: Protein, iron, B vitamins

8 tablespoons water 3 tablespoons dried lentils, washed	Bring water to boil. Simmer, covered until water is absorbed and lentils are tender, about 30 minutes. Mash with fork or blend in food processor until smooth.

Pea Puree

Primary nutrient: Potassium

Shell and wash peas if fresh. Bring 1 cup water to boil. Simmer peas, covered, until tender, about 5 to 10 minutes. Drain. Mash with fork or blend in food processor until smooth; add cooking water if necessary for consistency.

4 tablespoons peas, fresh or frozen

Potato Puree

Primary nutrient: Potassium

Boil the potato in the water, covered, 20 to 30 minutes. Drain. Mash with fork or use blender. Add formula or breast milk to thin.

1 medium potato, washed, peeled, and sliced into 1-inch pieces
2 cups water
Formula or breast milk

Spinach Puree

Primary nutrients: Iron, potassium, beta-carotene, folate (a B vitamin)

Boil or steam until tender, about 3 to 5 minutes. Drain. Blend in food processor until smooth; add cooking water if necessary for consistency.

4 or 5 leaves of spinach, washed, cut into 1-inch pieces

Brussels Sprouts Puree

Primary nutrients: Potassium, beta-carotene, vitamin C

5 small brussels sprouts, washed, outer leaves removed, and chopped

Boil or steam until tender, about 7 to 12 minutes. Drain. Mash with fork or blend in food processor until smooth; add cooking water if necessary for consistency.

Sweet Pepper Puree

Primary nutrients: Vitamin C

1 small red sweet pepper, washed, halved, and with seeds removed

Cut pepper into 1-inch sections. Boil or steam until tender, about 5 minutes. Drain. Mash with fork or blend in food processor until smooth; add cooking water if necessary for consistency.

Fruit Purees

When it's time, introduce these tasty purees . . . baby will think they are a real treat.

Banana

Primary nutrient: Potassium

Mash the banana with fork, or press the banana through a baby food grinder. You can add breast milk or formula to make a smoother consistency if desired.

½ ripe banana, peeled

■■

What's Going On in There?

Did you know a banana undergoes a major change as it ripens? When a banana is only partially ripe, one-third to one-half of its total carbohydrates are in the form of starches. By the time a banana is fully ripened, virtually all its carbohydrates will have magically transformed into simple sugars, making the banana soft and yummy sweet—just right for baby!

■■

Peach Puree

Primary nutrient: Potassium

Slice peach into quarters. Bring enough water to boil (just enough to cover peach). Cover and simmer until soft. Drain. Mash peach with fork or puree in blender with enough cooking water to make a smooth puree.

1 medium peach, washed, peeled, and pitted

Nursery Pears

Primary nutrients: Potassium, fiber

4 medium Anjou pears, washed, peeled, and quartered

Place pears in steamer basket with boiling water (enough to touch the bottom of the steamer basket). Cover tightly. Cook 8 to 12 minutes or until tender. Strain pears; puree. Serve cold.

Apple Puree

Primary nutrients: Potassium, vitamin C

1 medium apple, washed, peeled, core removed, and quartered

Put apple into saucepan with just enough water to cover apple. Bring to boil, cover, reduce heat, and simmer until soft. Drain. Mash apple with fork or puree in blender with enough cooking water to make a smooth puree.

Grape Puree

Primary nutrient: Potassium

8 green seedless grapes, washed with skins removed

Cut grapes in half. Mash with a fork.

Fig Puree

Primary nutrients: Calcium, potassium, magnesium, iron

Wash figs; soak overnight to soften. Bring water to boil (just enough to cover figs). Cover; simmer 10 to 20 minutes or until soft. Drain. Use food processor to blend.

4 dried figs
1 cup water for soaking and boiling

Second Foods

As you determine whether or not your baby has certain allergies, you can begin to make some simple mixes to add variety to baby's diet. Also keep in mind that children may need to be served food numerous times before accepting it—don't give up on nourishing foods!

Vegetables and Fruits: Popular Combinations

Some of these combinations may sound odd, but try them— your baby has no preconceived ideas of which foods should go together. These combinations are tasty and nutritious, too!

Mixed Vegetable Puree

Primary nutrients: Beta-carotene, vitamin C, potassium

1-pound bag of carrots, peeled and diced into chunks
1-pound bag of frozen green beans
1 medium zucchini, thickly sliced

Place carrots and green beans in steamer basket with boiling water (enough water to touch the bottom of the steamer basket). Cover tightly. Cook 6 to 7 minutes. Add zucchini and cook another 6 to 7 minutes until tender. Drain. Press through baby food grinder. Add liquid from cooking water to achieve smooth consistency.

Avocado-Banana Mix

Primary nutrients: Beta-carotene, potassium

½ avocado
½ banana
Breast milk or formula

Mash both avocado and banana with fork, or press through baby food grinder. Add breast milk or formula for the first few feedings.

Kiwi Banana

Primary nutrients: Potassium, vitamin C

1 ripe kiwi, peeled
1 ripe banana

Mash kiwi with fork. Mash banana. Mix the two together or puree in blender if baby needs a smooth texture.

Sweetie Pie Potatoes and Apples

Primary nutrients: Beta-carotene, vitamin C, fiber

Preheat oven to 350 degrees Fahrenheit. Place apples and sweet potatoes in buttered baking dish. Pour liquid over apples and sweet potatoes. Cover and bake 30 minutes or until soft. Puree and serve.

2 Washington Delicious apples, scrubbed well, cored, and sliced (I recommend using fresh apples with minimal wax coating.)

$3/4$ cup peeled sweet potato, cut into chunks

Butter

$1/4$ cup formula, breast milk, or water

Peachy Banana

Primary nutrients: Potassium, vitamin A, vitamin C

Place peach halves in a steamer basket in boiling water. Cover tightly. Cook 2 to 4 minutes. Strain. Blend in food processor with banana until pureed.

2 medium peaches, washed, peeled, pitted, and halved

1 ripe banana, peeled

Mango Banana

Primary nutrients: Beta-carotene, potassium, vitamin C

1 ripe banana
1 ripe mango, peeled and
  seeded
Breast milk or formula

Mash banana and mango with fork, or puree in blender. Add breast milk or formula to adjust consistency.

My Favorite Applesauce

Primary nutrient: Vitamin C

6 medium Golden Delicious
  apples, washed, cored, and
  quartered (I recommend
  fresh Washington apples with
  minimal wax coating.)
Cinnamon to taste

Place apples in a steamer basket above boiling water (enough water to touch the bottom of the steamer basket). Cover tightly. Cook 8 to 12 minutes or until apples are tender. Strain apples; remove skins. Keep 1 tablespoon of liquid to mix in moistness. Blend in food processor. Use a touch of cinnamon for flavor.

Cottage Cheese and Fruit

Primary nutrients: Beta-carotene, vitamin C, potassium, calcium

Place peach halves in a steamer basket in boiling water (enough water to touch the bottom of the steamer basket). Cover tightly. Cook 2 to 4 minutes. Strain. Add cottage cheese and reserved peach juice. Puree in food processor.

Variation: Use pears or apples in place of peaches.

2 medium peaches, washed, peeled, and pitted, with juice reserved

½ cup small-curd cottage cheese

Meats, Poultry, and Fish

Poultry provides an excellent source of iron and protein. You can begin introducing it at the six- to eight-month mark. You can use turkey and chicken that you have cooked for your family. Your main consideration is to keep this food free from spices (especially salt). Consider mixing poultry with cream of rice, breast milk, and butter. Combine poultry dishes with a little banana and breast milk to get a smoother consistency.

Chicken Banana Delight

Primary nutrients: Beta-carotene and protein

1 whole boneless chicken breast
cut into ³/₄-inch pieces
½ ripe banana

Remove visible chicken fat and any remaining skin. Be sure to look for and remove any bones. Boil chicken breast in pot of water for 20 minutes or until chicken is cooked through (the chicken will appear white when fully cooked). Strain; keep ½ cup of the chicken broth. Puree chicken in food processor. Add banana and some broth to make a smooth, creamy consistency.

Chicken and Rice

Primary nutrients: Protein, B vitamins, iron

4 cups water
2 cups rice (try Japanese short-
grain white rice)
1 pound boneless, skinless
chicken breast

Bring four cups of water to a boil in a medium saucepan. Add rice, stir briefly, cover, and cook until water is absorbed and rice is tender. Remove visible chicken fat. Be sure to look for and remove any bones, just in case. Boil chicken breast in a pot of water for 20 minutes or until chicken is cooked through. Strain; keep ½ cup of the broth. Puree chicken in food processor; add cooked rice. Add broth as needed to make a smooth, creamy consistency. I prefer to boil chicken for tenderness and to protect against any risk of salmonella bacteria contamination.

Chicken and Carrots

Primary nutrients: Beta-carotene, protein, iron

Place carrots in a steamer basket with boiling water (enough water to touch the bottom of the steamer basket). Cover tightly. Cook 12 to 14 minutes. Strain. Puree in baby food grinder. Add water 1 tablespoon at a time as needed. Remove visible fat from the chicken. Be sure to look for and remove any bones, just in case. Boil chicken breast in pot of water for 20 minutes or until cooked through. Strain; keep ½ cup of the broth for blending. Puree chicken in food processor. Blend chicken and carrots together, adding broth as needed until smooth and creamy.

1-pound bag of carrots, peeled and cut into chunks
1 whole boneless, skinless chicken breast

Turkey-Banana Puree

Primary nutrients: Iron, potassium, protein

To prepare the turkey, remove visible turkey fat and any remaining skin. Be sure to look for and remove any bones. Place turkey into boiling water and cook for 20 minutes or until turkey is cooked through. Strain; keep 1 cup of the broth. Puree turkey in processor and add banana. Use remaining broth for a smooth, creamy texture.

1 whole boneless turkey breast cut into ¾-inch pieces
½ ripe banana, peeled

Turkey and Peas

Primary nutrients: Protein, iron, potassium

One 10-ounce package of frozen
    peas (baby peas work best)
1 whole boneless turkey breast

Place peas in steamer basket with boiling water (enough water to touch the bottom of the steamer basket). Cook 3 to 8 minutes until tender. Strain. Press through baby food grinder to puree. Add water as needed. Place turkey into boiling water and cook 20 minutes or until turkey is cooked through. Strain; keep 1 cup of the broth. Blend turkey and peas together with extra broth until smooth and creamy. *Variation:* Use any vegetable or ½ cup cooked rice as a substitute for peas.

Turkey and Gravy

Primary nutrients: Protein, iron, calcium

1 whole boneless turkey breast,
    cut into ¾-inch pieces
8 ounces breast milk or formula
½ teaspoon cornstarch

Remove visible turkey fat and any remaining skin. Be sure to look for and remove any bones. Place turkey into boiling water and cook 10 minutes or until turkey is cooked through. Strain; keep 1 cup of the broth. Puree turkey in processor; add milk or formula and cornstarch. Use a little of the remaining broth for a smooth, creamy texture.

Timesaving Recipes

For some parents, these timesaving recipes will be a real help.

Show 'em what you've got. This is where you can get creative while making baby food in quantity. Experiment by creating recipe variations from a base fruit (such as apples) or a vegetable (such as potatoes). The following recipes are designed so you can make them all at once. For example, you will cook 12 apples, enough to use in all three apple recipes. To make all the potato recipes, you would start by cooking 12 potatoes. To prevent food-borne illness, refrigerate only what you expect to use within two to three days; freeze the rest.

Types of Apples

Braeburn:	Combination of tart and sweet flavors.
Criterion:	Sweet. Good for making candy apples.
Elstar:	Sweet, tangy flavor. Good for snacking, fruit trays.
Fuji:	Sweet, mild, crisp, and juicy. Good for cooking. Store well.
Gala:	Sweet, aromatic, rich flavor. Good for salads.
Golden Delicious:	Rich, mellow flavor. Considered an all-purpose apple.
Granny Smith:	Tart and crisp. Good for sautéing, baking.
Jonagold:	Outstanding sweet, tart flavor. Good for salads and baking.
Jonathan:	Moderately tart with a rich, distinctive flavor. Good for cooking.
Red Delicious:	Mild, sweet. Good for garnishes and snacking.
Rome Beauty:	Primarily a cooking apple. Good for baked apples.
Winesap:	Spicy, juicy flavor. Good for ciders.

Base Ingredient: Apples

Use Fuji apples for best results in the following recipes.

Basic Applesauce

Primary nutrients: Vitamin C, soluble fiber

12 Fuji apples, peeled and
    cored
1 quart water

Boil apples in 1 quart water. Take 6 apples and puree in blender. Yields 6 cups applesauce.

Fun Facts About Apples

There are 2,500 varieties of apples grown in the United States.

Apples grow in all fifty states.

Apples are fat free.

The Delicious variety is the most widely grown in the United States.

Europe, France, Italy, and Germany are the leading apple-producing countries.

Apples are a great source of fiber.

Apples are a member of the rose family.

Carrots and Applesauce

The apples add a nice flavor to the carrots, so this mixture is helpful if your baby does not like carrots.

Primary nutrients: Beta-carotene, potassium, vitamin C

Boil or steam carrots; drain. Boil apples in water. Puree carrots with apples.

1-pound bag baby carrots, peeled and cut into chunks
3 apples
1 quart water

Apples and Bananas

Primary nutrients: Potassium, vitamin C

Boil apples in water. Mix bananas with cooked apples. Three days of food, ready to go!

3 apples
4 bananas
1 quart water

Base Ingredient: Potatoes

Potatoes are indeed vegetables, but they are so rich in starch that they sometimes take the place of grains. When serving potatoes, include a non-starchy vegetable with the meal, too. In all of these recipes, leave the skins on the potatoes and use White Rose, Red, Pontiac, or blue/purple when in season. (See sidebar on page 116 for explanation.)

Fun Facts About Potatoes

The United States grows about 35 billion pounds of potatoes every year.

Potatoes are the most popular vegetable among Americans.

Potatoes are high in vitamin C and potassium, and are a good source of fiber.

Potato Blend

Primary nutrients: Potassium, niacin (a B vitamin)

12 large potatoes

3 quarts water

Breast milk or formula

Boil potatoes 30 minutes in water until tender (pierce with fork to check). Cool under cold water and peel. Blend 3 potatoes with small mixture of formula or breast milk to a smooth consistency.

What Is a Leek?

The leek is a member of the allium family—better known as the onion family. A favorite of the Romans and the Greeks to soothe a sore throat, the leek became Emperor Nero's favorite vegetable. Leeks are best when they are boiled. They make great flavoring when combined with potatoes as part of your baby's first foods.

Potatoes and Leeks

Primary nutrients: Potassium, niacin

Boil potatoes 30 minutes in water until tender (pierce with fork to check). Cut leeks lengthwise through almost all layers. Spread open and wash thoroughly to remove all sand. Cut off all green stems (use white part only). Boil leeks 15 minutes in separate pot of water. Blend 2 of the leeks and potatoes in processor (use water from leeks to make blended consistency).

2 potatoes
3 leeks

Potatoes, Leeks, and Peas

Primary nutrients: Vitamin C, potassium

Place peas, remaining leek (prepared as in above recipe) and 2 potatoes (prepared as in above recipe) in blender. Puree.

8 ounces of frozen baby petite peas
2 potatoes
1 leek

Potatoes and Broccoli

Primary nutrients: Potassium, vitamin C, beta-carotene

Place broccoli into a steamer basket and cook 8 to 11 minutes (with enough water to reach the bottom of the steamer basket). Pierce with fork to determine tenderness. Blend with 2 potatoes (prepared as in above recipe). Reserve water from broccoli to make smooth puree.

1 broccoli bunch, stalks
   removed, head cut into
   florets
2 potatoes

Potatoes and Zucchini

Primary nutrient: Potassium

2 medium zucchini, washed and cut into 1/4-inch rounds
2 potatoes

Place zucchini into a steamer basket (with enough boiling water to reach the bottom of the basket); cook 7 to 11 minutes. Pierce with fork to determine tenderness. Blend in with 2 potatoes (prepared as in above recipe). Reserve water from zucchini to make smooth puree.

Types of Potatoes

Blue, Purple:	Available mostly in the fall. The flesh ranges in color from dark blue or lavender to white. These potatoes have a delicate, nutty flavor and are best microwaved, steamed, or baked.
Katahdin:	All-purpose potatoes. These are white, oval potatoes that are great for steaming, baking, and roasting.
Red Pontiac:	Round red, smooth-skinned potatoes that are white inside, with a firm texture. They are good for boiling, steaming, or baking.
Russet Burbank:	These are oblong and dark-skinned. Best baked or mashed.
White Rose:	They are oblong, and good for boiling, roasting, or baking.
Yellow Flesh:	Available in summer and fall. Have a milky, buttery flavor. Best baked or mashed.

Vegetable-Ham Dinner

Primary nutrients: Potassium, beta-carotene, iron, protein

Boil or steam green beans and carrots until tender, about 12 to 14 minutes. Drain. Add cooked potato (prepared as in previous recipe) and ham. Put in food processor. Add liquid from vegetables to achieve smooth consistency.

1 pound fresh green beans, washed and cut in ¼-inch pieces

1 pound of carrots, peeled and cut into chunks

1 potato

2 ounces of cooked ham (sliced is good to work with), cut into ¼-inch pieces

Foods for the Teething Baby

Teething usually begins in the sixth month of your baby's life and continues on and off until age three.

What to look for. Some of the signs that herald teething are mild irritability, crying, low-grade fever, excessive drooling, and a desire to chew on something hard. You will also notice your baby's gums looking red and swollen. In most children, the two bottom front teeth appear first, followed by four upper teeth (central and lateral incisors) in the next four to eight weeks.

Non-edible solutions. Teething rings—kept cold in the refrigerator—are helpful and offer temporary relief. Medications are very short-lived, as they tend to wash out of the baby's mouth as quickly as you put them on. Some mothers use oil of cloves, rubbed on the gums in *tiny* amounts. The oil keeps the "active" ingredient on baby's gums for a short time.

Teething biscuits. At this time, baby strongly desires something hard to chew on. Hard items such as teething biscuits dissolve slowly and keep baby gnawing—just what's needed to help those teeth break through the gums. You might also try zwieback or arrowroot cookies from the baby food aisle, or make your own teething "biscuits." Do this by purchasing rice bread (or other non-wheat bread) at a natural-food store. Toast slices lightly. Cut slices into one-inch strips, lay on cookie sheet, and toast in low oven (250 degrees Fahrenheit) until hard.

Mother knows best. I can't go much further without recommending my mother's Greek koulouria recipe. In the Greek Orthodox tradition, these cookies are baked on Holy Thursday before Easter. Special ingredients in koulouria make the cookies unique and very tasty for baby after her first birthday or while teething! These ingredients are vanillin and mastica. Purchase them at a delicatessen or specialty food store. You can store these cookies for at least a month in an airtight container. You will enjoy this recipe so much, I'm sure you'll make it for yourself as a coffee treat.

Koulouria

This recipe is recommended for children over one year of age.
Primary nutrients: Protein, fat, calcium, B vitamins

Preheat oven to 400 degrees F. In large mixing bowl, cream butter and powdered sugar until light and fluffy. Add eggs one at a time, blending well. In another mixing bowl, mix 4 cups of the flour (best results if sifted) with vanillin, baking powder, salt, and mastica. Add flour mixture to butter mixture. Fold in evaporated milk. Add remaining 1 cup of flour to make a stiff dough. Mix with your hand. If you find the dough is too sticky, add more flour. Refrigerate half an hour. Remove. To roll cookies, pinch off dough about a tablespoon at a time, and on a wooden surface, roll out to 5-inch length. Double over into hairpin shape. Twist two sides together. Place on ungreased baking sheet about 1 inch apart. Whisk beaten egg with milk until blended. Brush with egg mixture. Bake 10 to 12 minutes or until golden brown. Cool and harden before giving to baby to enjoy.

½ pound butter, softened
3½ cups powdered sugar
6 eggs
5 cups white flour, sifted
2 teaspoons powdered vanillin
2 teaspoons baking powder
½ teaspoon salt
½ teaspoon mastica (ground)
One 5-ounce can evaporated
  milk

For basting spread:
1 egg, beaten
1 teaspoon whole milk

CHAPTER 7

More of the Best Foods: Intermediate Recipes

No one who cooks, cooks alone. Even at her most solitary, a cook in the kitchen is surrounded by generations of cooks past, the advice and menus of cooks present, the wisdom of cookbook writers.
—Laurie Colwin, from the book *Simple Abundance*

Once your baby has been safely introduced to solids and is less dependent on breast milk or formula, it's time to progress to a more varied diet. Since babies grow and change so quickly, this chapter further divides the "intermediate" stage that covers the latter half of the first year to help you gradually introduce the most appropriate foods.

Seven to Ten Months

Feeding becomes more fun. You can introduce more than a dozen new foods to babies between seven and nine months of age. Your baby may be ready for foods with more texture. You may notice that your baby begins to chew with better up-and-down movement of the jaw, replacing the sucking motion. You will also notice how she grasps bottles and other objects. Her bottom two teeth are probably in, and her top two teeth are ready to break through. These are signs that your baby is ready for finger food that she can actually chew on.

Keeping a balance. Once your baby is getting more and more of his nutrition from solids and less from breast milk or formula, you'll need to replace the nutrients he's no longer receiving. For example, the food you introduce now should offer some protein and calcium. See the sidebar on page 122 for examples.

By seven months, most babies are familiar with being spoon-fed. They are ready to begin eating different vegetable-and-cereal combinations, yogurt, and other foods. They also need protein, either from meats and fish or a combination of legumes with grains to get complete protein.

Making the change. As he makes the transition from seven to nine months into ten to twelve months, your baby will further decrease his number of feedings from the bottle or breast and begin to eat soft or finely chopped table foods

Teething biscuits, toast, bagels, and crackers are easy for your baby to hold. (See chapter 6 for ideas on teething biscuits and the recipe for koulouria, a hard cookie that I recommend for teething babies.) Some research has shown that it is critical to offer harder-to-chew foods at this developmental age. If you don't, you may have problems getting a baby to accept them later.

(without added salt or sugar). Use the following as a guideline in determining how much to feed your baby—but keep in mind that baby knows best when he's hungry and when he's full—it's your job to pay attention to him.

Foods for Babies Seven to Nine Months Old

Begin to make the foods less smooth, leaving a few soft chunks so baby can experience chewing, or gumming, her food. Now is also the time to let baby begin feeding herself finger foods and trying her own hand at a small spoon. Here's a list to get you started:

- Mashed, rather than pureed, vegetables and fruit—either soft, ripe, or cooked
- Cooked vegetable strips or slices
- Peeled, soft fruit wedges or slices
- Strained or finely chopped protein foods such as meat, chicken, fish, and beans
- Plain yogurt
- Cheese cubes
- Tofu
- Cooked, mashed egg yolk
- Brown rice
- More varieties of cereals and grains, such as mixed grains and wheat (Try toast squares, unsalted soda crackers, and soft tortillas.)
- Calcium-enriched formulas to supplement regular formula feedings

Breads and cereals from the table, plus infant cereal: 4 or more servings

Vegetables: 3 servings

Fruits: 2 servings

Protein (meat, fish, poultry, eggs, legumes, tofu): 2 servings

Breast milk or formula: 16 to 24 ounces

Note: Serving sizes for babies are smaller than for adults. For instance, use one-half slice of bread instead of a whole slice, or one-fourth cup rice or noodles instead of half a cup. The "tablespoon per year of age" as a serving size can also apply although many babies will be happy to eat more than that.

Now let's get going on some intermediate foods for your soon-to-be toddler.

Soupy Soups!

Soups are a great way to get nutritious food and warmth into your baby. Here are several nutritious soups your baby will enjoy. Each recipe makes 2 to 4 servings.

Creamy Vegetable Soup

Primary nutrients: Calcium, beta-carotene

Place vegetables in a steamer basket with a small amount of boiling water. Cover. Cook 8 to 12 minutes or until veggies are tender. Strain, reserving 1 tablespoon of liquid to add for consistency. Puree veggies, chicken broth, and milk in food processor. Serve warm.

1 cup diced carrots
1 cup green beans, stems cut
½ cup cooked potato
1½ cups chicken broth
¾ cup formula or breast milk

Split Pea and Ham Soup

Primary nutrients: Vitamin A, protein

1 pound dried split green peas, rinsed

8 cups water

1 small onion, peeled

1 bay leaf

8 ounces cooked ham, cubed

Put peas in large cooking pot with 8 cups water. Add onion and bay leaf. Bring to boil, then reduce to simmer. Cook 1 to 2 hours, until creamy. Add ham during last 15 minutes of cooking. Puree in blender for a thick, smooth soup. Serve warm.

Hint of Mint Soup

Primary nutrients: Vitamins A and C

2/3 cup frozen petite peas

1/2 cup fresh green beans, stems off, washed

Sprig of fresh mint, washed thoroughly

Place vegetables in a steamer basket with a small amount of boiling water. Cover. Cook 8 to 12 minutes or until veggies are tender, adding mint sprig during last 2 to 3 minutes of steaming. Strain. Keep 1 tablespoon of liquid to add for consistency. Puree veggies and mint in food processor. Serve warm.

Peanut Butter Soup

If there are no peanut allergies in your family, this might be a good way to try peanut butter on your baby, as the peanut butter is diluted with other ingredients. If peanut butter soup sounds strange to you, think of it as a thin, Asian peanut sauce—yummm!

Primary nutrients: Protein, calcium, and vitamin D (if fortified cow's milk is used)

Melt butter over medium heat in saucepan. Remove pan from heat, and add flour and peanut butter. Return to medium heat and slowly add milk or formula, stirring constantly, until boiling. Serve warm.

Variation: Add cooked carrots and blend until smooth. Carrots go well with the peanut butter flavor.

2 tablespoons butter
1 tablespoon flour
1/4 cup peanut butter
2 cups breast milk or formula

Golden Carrot-Rice Soup

Primary nutrients: Beta-carotene, B-vitamins, fiber

Place rice and carrots in saucepan with water and cover. Simmer until water has absorbed (about 30 minutes). Puree in blender with butter, until smooth. Serve warm.

2 tablespoons brown rice, uncooked
6 carrots, peeled and washed
1 1/3 cups water
1/2 teaspoon unsalted butter

Tasty Carrot-Bean Soup

Primary nutrients: Beta-carotene, protein

1 carrot, peeled and chopped
¼ cup cooked navy beans
1 cup water

Place ingredients with 1 cup water in covered saucepan. Simmer until tender. Puree in food processor. Serve warm.

Mixed Dishes

It's fun to introduce new flavors to your baby by making different food combinations. Here are some recipes to get you started.

Sweet Potato and Chicken Dinner

Primary nutrients: Beta-carotene, protein

One 8-ounce skinless, boneless
  chicken breast
1 small sweet potato, peeled,
  cut into 1-inch pieces
¼ cup low-sodium chicken
  broth

Cut chicken into small pieces. Place ingredients into pot with enough water to cover. Simmer, covered, 30 minutes. Puree in food processor. Use additional broth if needed for smooth consistency. Serve warm.

Pureed Lentil-Rice Pilaf

Primary nutrients: Protein, iron, B vitamins

Blend lentils and rice together, and puree with a little formula or breast milk for consistency. Serve warm.

¼ cup cooked lentils
¾ cup cooked brown rice
Breast milk or formula

Chicken Delight

Primary nutrients: Protein, vitamin A

Remove visible fat and any remaining skin from chicken. Be sure to look for and remove any bones. Boil chicken breast in pot of water for 20 minutes or until cooked through. Strain, reserving ½ cup of the broth. Puree chicken with cooked veggies in food processor, adding enough broth for a smooth, creamy consistency. Serve warm.

1 whole boneless chicken breast cut into ¾-inch pieces
1 potato, peeled, cooked, and quartered
1 carrot, peeled, cooked, and diced
½ zucchini, washed, sliced, and cooked
½ celery stalk, washed, cooked, and cut into 1-inch slices

Fragrant Winter Squash

Primary nutrients: Beta-carotene, potassium

1 acorn or butternut squash,
washed, halved, seeds
discarded
Pinch of ground cinnamon or
cloves
Formula or breast milk

Preheat oven to 350 degrees F. Place squash cut side down on foil-lined baking sheet. Bake 45 minutes to 1 hour. Pierce with fork to check for softness. Cool, then peel or scoop out of shell. Add spice; puree in food processor, adding formula or breast milk for smooth consistency. Serve warm.

Spring Vegetables and Pasta

Primary nutrients: Vitamins A and C, carbohydrates

½ cup fresh green beans,
washed and tips removed
½ cup peeled baby carrots
½ cup petite peas
½ cup green zucchini, washed
and sliced (peel on)
1 cup cooked pasta of choice

Place green beans and carrots in steamer basket with small amount of boiling water. Cover. Cook about 4 minutes then add peas and zucchini. Cook another 4 to 8 minutes or until tender. Strain, reserving 1 tablespoon of liquid to add for consistency. Puree veggies and pasta in processor. Serve warm.

Egg Yolk

This is a good way to introduce eggs to your baby.
Primary nutrients: Protein, vitamin A

Place egg in small saucepan and cover with water.
Bring to boil. Simmer 7 minutes. Drain, run under
cool water. Peel egg, discard white. Mash yolk with
fork, adding formula or milk to make the yolk
creamy.

1 egg
A few drops of formula or milk

Baby's First Omelet

Primary nutrients: Protein, calcium, vitamin A

With fork, blend yolk and milk in bowl. Melt butter in small skillet over low heat. Pour egg mixture
into skillet, and cook until firm. Sprinkle with
cheese, fold in half and cover until cheese melts.
Cool slightly then serve.

1 egg yolk
1 tablespoon formula or breast
   milk
1 teaspoon unsalted butter
2 tablespoons grated Cheddar
   cheese

Tropical Twist Yogurt

Primary nutrient: Vitamin D

3 tablespoons finely grated
    carrot
3 tablespoons finely chopped
    pineapple
3 tablespoons plain yogurt

Blend all; serve cold.

Ten to Twelve Months

You will see a big difference during this stage. Your baby may be grabbing and moving around more than ever. She's ready to start feeding herself!

What does this mean? Breast milk and formula are still important, but they begin to take a backseat now as your baby moves on to table foods. When recipe instructions call for pureeing in this section, do so with a light touch. Just puree the food slightly, leaving more and more soft chunks as baby's feeding skills progress.

Such a variety now. More protein-rich foods—such as tender, moist, cooked lean meats and chopped egg yolk—are good choices now. By the end of the first year, regular dairy products can also become a part of your baby's diet. Baby should be able to eat many adult foods, as long as they are served at a texture and consistency that she can swallow.

Foods for Ten- to Twelve-Month-Olds

It's okay to include these foods now, if you haven't already.

Finger Foods	Protein Foods
Small pieces of ripe peeled fruit	Egg yolk
Soft-cooked fruits and vegetables	Lean meat
Dry, low-sugar cereal (such as bran flakes)	Fish or poultry
Pasta and noodles	Dried cooked legumes
Breads and muffins	Tofu
	Cow's milk
	Soft cheese

Safety is still an issue. Just watch for foods that may be a choking hazard, including nuts, seeds, popcorn, whole grapes, hot dogs, raw vegetables—especially large or round pieces—and even peanut butter. Peanuts and peanut butter may also cause allergies, so you may want to wait until baby is older (age two or three) before serving them, especially if peanut allergies run in your family. The end of this section includes several recipes that call for peanut butter, but use your own judgment as to whether to serve them to your baby.

Keep it as natural as you can. Serving foods closest to their natural state is best. That way food retains more of its original nutrients and fewer added and unnecessary ingredients such as chemical colorings, flavorings, and preservatives, or unwanted salt, fat, and sugar. For example, tender cooked ground

Time to Introduce Liver!

You may first give your baby liver at ten months. Liver is a great source of vitamins A and B complex, protein, and iron. Do not serve liver more than once a week, however, because it contains large amounts of iron, and your baby may overload on iron. I suggest introducing liver with a vegetable puree first.

beef is better than a hot dog, and soft-cooked potato wedges are better than chips. It's also a good idea to remove enough food for baby from the family cooking pot before adding salt, heavy or hot spices, or sugar. Your baby doesn't need these flavor enhancers—he thinks Mother Nature does it just fine!

Combination Dishes

Chicken Liver and Avocado

Primary nutrients: Protein, iron, zinc, vitamin A

1 chicken liver, cleaned and trimmed

1 cup chicken stock

¼ ripe avocado, pitted

Formula or breast milk

Cook chicken liver with chicken stock 10 minutes over low heat. Place in blender with avocado. Puree, adding breast milk or formula as necessary for a smooth consistency. Serve at room temperature.

Fruity Rice

Primary nutrients: Potassium, vitamins C and B complex, fiber

Cook apples in water until soft, reserving some of water for pureeing. Puree in blender with remaining ingredients.

2 apples, cored and peeled
6 ripe plums, washed and pitted
2 bananas, peeled and sliced
$1/4$ cup cooked brown rice

Apple-Plum Delight

Primary nutrients: Vitamin C, potassium

Boil apple in water (enough to cover) until tender. Reserve water. Blend plum and apple in food processor. Add reserved water as necessary for smooth consistency.

1 medium Red Delicious apple, peeled and quartered
1 plum, washed and pitted

Peach-Apricot Muesli

Primary nutrients: Protein, beta-carotene, potassium, calcium, fiber

½ cup fresh peaches, washed, cut, and pitted

½ cup fresh apricots, washed, cut, and pitted

2 tablespoons chopped dates

1 cup breast milk, water, or formula

3 tablespoons ground millet

¼ cup ground oats (sold at natural foods stores)

Puree peaches, apricots, and dates. In saucepan, bring liquid to a boil. Sprinkle in millet and oats, stirring constantly. Simmer 10 minutes until soft and most of liquid is absorbed. Add puree to millet and oats. Cook several minutes more until warmed through. Serve.

Pureed Pea and Brown Rice Pilaf

Primary nutrients: Vitamin C, carbohydrates

One 16-ounce bag frozen petite peas

¼ cup cooked brown rice

Boil peas 2 minutes in 1 quart water. Drain. Puree rice and peas in blender.

Magnificent Macaroni

Primary nutrients: Vitamin C, protein

Sauté beef at medium temperature in skillet with olive oil until brown and thoroughly cooked (no pink), 5 to 8 minutes. Add fresh tomatoes, sauce, parsley, and cheese to skillet. Cook 10 minutes. Puree. Serve with cooked macaroni.

¼ pound lean ground beef

2 tablespoons extra-virgin olive oil

3 vine-ripened tomatoes, washed and chopped

One 15-ounce can tomato sauce

1 tablespoon chopped fresh parsley

3 tablespoons freshly grated Parmesan cheese

½ pound egg-free elbow macaroni, cooked

Vegetable and Fruit Dishes

Baby will like these vegetables and fruits, tasty and delicious—and you'll like how easy they are to make!

Summer Corn Treat

Primary nutrient: Potassium

Husk corn, and wash off silk. Boil in water 10 minutes or until cooked. Using knife, scrape corn off cob. Puree with rice flour in blender, adding formula or breast milk to achieve smooth consistency.

6 ears fresh corn

3 tablespoons rice flour

Formula or breast milk for mixing

Great Green Beans

Primary nutrients: Potassium, beta-carotene

6 ounces fresh green beans, washed, stems removed, and cut into ½-inch pieces

Put beans into a steamer basket set in a pot of boiling water (enough water to touch bottom of steamer basket). Cover tightly and steam 10 to 12 minutes. Puree in blender.

Garden Vegetable Delight

Primary nutrients: Vitamin C, beta-carotene, potassium

1 cup fresh green beans, washed, with ends removed
1 cup baby carrots, washed and peeled
½ cup cooked potato

Place carrots and green beans in steamer basket with boiling water (enough to touch bottom of steamer basket). Cook, covered, 8 to 12 minutes or until tender. Strain, reserving one tablespoon liquid to add for consistency. Puree veggies with potato in processor. Serve warm.

Vegetable Purees Most Frequently Made

These recipes are for small servings and offer easy preparation.

Bright Beet Puree

Primary nutrient: Potassium

Leave a small portion of stalk and root on beet, so it does not "bleed" while cooking. Bring to boil in 2 cups water. Simmer until tender, about 30 minutes to 1 hour depending on size of beet. Drain. Cool until you can handle beet. Remove skin. Mash with fork until smooth. (Beets may show up as red in your baby's stool or urine. This is harmless.)

1 small beet, scrubbed well
2 cups water for cooking

Tantalizing Tomatoes

Avoid acidic foods such as tomatoes if baby has sore gums—they can cause a stinging and burning sensation.

Primary nutrients: Potassium, beta-carotene, vitamin C

Bring 2 cups water to boil. Put tomato into boiling water for 1 minute. Drain. Remove skin. Mash with fork, or process until smooth.

1 small tomato, washed
2 cups water for cooking

Teddy's Turnip Puree

Primary nutrient: Potassium

Bring 1 cup water to boil. Simmer turnip, covered, 15 to 20 minutes until tender. Mash with fork, or process until smooth, adding cooking water as needed for consistency.

1 small turnip, washed, scrubbed, and peeled
1 cup water for cooking

> Fantastic Fruits
>
> Again, these purees are for small servings and offer quick and easy preparation.

Grapefruit Puree

Primary nutrients: Vitamin C, potassium

½ small grapefruit, peeled, membrane and skin removed, quartered

1 cup apple juice

Blend grapefruit in blender with apple juice. If the grapefruit is particularly sour, you may need to add ½ teaspoon sugar, but let baby try it first. Sour can be interesting!

Jubilee Cantaloupe

Primary nutrients: Beta-carotene, vitamin C, potassium

1 medium cantaloupe, cut into eighths, rind and seeds removed

Wash rind of cantaloupe thoroughly before cutting to avoid transferring any harmful bacteria from the rind into the flesh of the melon. Place cantaloupe pieces in steamer basket with enough water to reach the bottom of the basket. Steam, covered, 2 to 3 minutes. Drain. Puree.

Nifty Nectarine Puree

Primary nutrients: Potassium, beta-carotene, niacin (a B vitamin)

Place nectarines in a steamer basket over boiling water. Steam, covered, 2 to 3 minutes. Drain. Puree.

4 medium nectarines, washed, peeled, halved, and pitted

Peanut Butter-Banana Pudding

Primary nutrients: Protein, potassium

Blend all in food processor. Serve at room temperature.

2 tablespoons peanut butter
2 tablespoons applesauce
1/2 banana

Tempting Banana-Tofu Pudding

Primary nutrients: Protein, potassium

Blend all ingredients in food processor. Add formula or breast milk as necessary for a smooth consistency. Serve at room temperature or chilled as a pudding.

2 tablespoons peanut butter
2 tablespoons silken tofu
1/2 banana
Formula or breast milk

CHAPTER 8

Recipes from Experienced Chefs and Parents

Experience isn't interesting until it begins to repeat itself—
in fact, till it does that, it hardly is experience.
—Elizabeth Bowen, *The Death of the Heart*

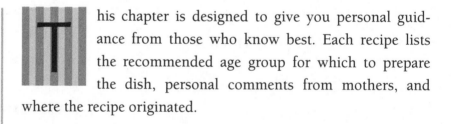

his chapter is designed to give you personal guidance from those who know best. Each recipe lists the recommended age group for which to prepare the dish, personal comments from mothers, and where the recipe originated.

Sweet Potato Surprise

Salt Lake City, Utah

Age group: 6 months and up

Experienced chef: Cyndia T. Cayias

Special comments: "This dish looks and smells like a crisp autumn day!"

Boil sweet potatoes and apples in water until soft but not mushy, (about 20 minutes). Remove; pat dry. Mash until creamy, slowly adding juices. Add cinnamon to taste, blending all ingredients. Serve warm.

Tip: Citrus fruits are a common allergen. Before including orange juice in a recipe such as this one, make sure you've served orange juice to your baby beforehand with no adverse effects.

1 to 2 medium sweet potatoes, peeled and quartered

1 to 2 medium Red Delicious apples, peeled and quartered

2 tablespoons pineapple juice

2 tablespoons orange juice

Cinnamon

Fresh Vegetable Casserole with Chicken

Toledo, Ohio

Age group: 6 to 8 months

Experienced chef: Lambrini Linardakis

Special comments: "Before you start preparing baby's food, wash your hands carefully, and wash cooking equipment in hot water and rinse well. Use a clean cutting board and knife to cut vegetables into small pieces. Boil or steam together until tender. Mash cooked vegetables with a fork or blend into a puree and serve."

¼ pound skinless chicken breast
½ cup carrots, peeled and cut
½ cup peas
½ cup spinach
½ cup potatoes, peeled and cut
4 cups broth

Place chicken in saucepan and add enough water to cover. Boil 30 to 45 minutes or until tender. Remove chicken. Add vegetables to 4 cups of the previously prepared broth. Bring to boil. Cut chicken in small pieces, and add to vegetable-broth mixture. Continue boiling until vegetables are tender. Puree in food processor.

Apple-Chicken Medley

Salt Lake City, Utah

Age group: 7 months and older

Experienced chef: Ernestine Pippas

Special comments: "This recipe can be served to your baby while making a slight variation for the family dinner. Chicken is an excellent source of protein and goes very well with the apples."

Boil or steam apples in 1 cup water until tender, (about 5 minutes). Drain. Place apples and remaining ingredients in blender or food processor and puree.

½ cup peeled, sliced apples

1 cup water

½ cup shredded and cooked white chicken (this is equivalent to a 3-ounce skinless, boneless chicken breast)

⅓ cup cooked brown rice

½ cup breast milk or formula

Grandma Parson's Vegetable Soup

Salt Lake City, Utah

Age group: 8 to 12 months

Experienced chef: Rachel Jones

Special comments: "This soup is a favorite for all family members and especially for younger ones. It is a good source of vitamin A, vitamin C, and fiber. We have added cooked squash and hamburger to this recipe for a different flavor, and hamburger increases the iron and protein content of the soup."

4 cups tomato sauce

2 carrots, peeled and chopped

2 celery stalks, chopped

2 potatoes, peeled and cubed

1 small onion, chopped

1 cup uncooked corkscrew pasta

1 tablespoon brown sugar

1 tablespoon apple cider
  vinegar

2 tablespoons dried basil

1 tablespoon dried oregano

1 beef bouillon cube

Place tomato sauce in a saucepan over medium heat. Add all other ingredients. Add enough water to cover ingredients; bring to boil. Reduce heat, and simmer 35 to 40 minutes, stirring occasionally.

Earth Meets Sky Jubilee

Chicago, Illinois

Age group: 9 months and older

Experienced chef: Mee Kim-Chavez

Special comments: "I like to combine the earthy flavors of root vegetables with the apples that reach for the sky—they go together well."

Simmer carrots, beets, parsley, and apple in apple juice until all are tender, (about 10 minutes). Puree in blender.

2 medium carrots, peeled and sliced

2 small beets, cooked and diced

1 tablespoon finely chopped fresh parsley

½ apple, washed, cored and diced

⅓ cup 100% pure apple juice

Chicken Tonight . . . Soup Tomorrow

Chicago, Illinois

Age group: 9 to 12 months

Experienced chef: Antigone Polite

Special comments: "V-8 juice is the secret ingredient used for zip and nutrition. Both meals may be refrigerated for later. Eat within 48 hours. Warm up with a little water to loosen."

1½ cups water

4-ounce boneless chicken breast, cubed

¼ teaspoon minced garlic (optional)

½ teaspoon minced onion (optional)

½ carrot, peeled and cut

½ potato, peeled and cut

½ cup zucchini, squash, or green beans

½ cup low-sodium V-8 juice

In medium saucepan, in 1½ cups water, boil chicken and spices 10 minutes. Add veggies and boil 7 to 10 minutes or until tender. Drain, reserving liquid. Add V-8 juice. Bring to boil. Puree veggies in blender to consistency palatable for child, adding warm water as needed. *Tomorrow's meal:* Use reserved liquid to boil rice or to use with baby rice to make mush. Blend to baby's preferred consistency.

Georgia's Favorite Veal and Veggies

Salt Lake City, Utah

Age group: 9 to 12 months

Experienced chef: Nitsa Tsoutsounis

Special comments: "You can also make this recipe with chicken instead of veal. If you do, use chicken drumsticks (dark meat), because of their high iron content."

Put meat and vegetables in saucepan with enough water to cover. Boil until tender, about 20 to 30 minutes. Puree all ingredients in blender. Serve warm. You can also use chicken for your own meal.

5 ounces veal, trimmed of all fat

2 carrots, peeled and chopped

2 medium potatoes, peeled and chopped

A few green beans, ends and strings removed, chopped

1 medium tomato, coarsely chopped

3 sprigs broccoli, chopped

Carrot and Apple Pancakes

Port Sanilac, Michigan

Age group: 9 to 12 months

Experienced chef: Susan Klimala

Special comments: "This is a good way to add important fruits and veggies. You could also substitute zucchini and/or pears, depending on what your baby likes."

¾ cup all-purpose flour

1 cup whole wheat flour

¼ teaspoon salt

1¾ teaspoons baking powder

6 tablespoons apple juice
   concentrate

2 egg yolks, lightly beaten

4 tablespoons melted butter

1¼ cups breast milk or formula

¾ cup apple, peeled and grated

¾ cup grated carrot

Combine flours, salt, and baking powder in a bowl. In separate bowl, mix juice concentrate, egg yolks, butter, and milk or formula. Pour liquid into flour mixture. Stir to smooth consistency. Stir in grated apple and carrot. Spoon batter onto hot griddle to make cakes about 3 inches across. Flip when surface bubbles and edges appear dry. Serve with applesauce, plain yogurt, or a little maple syrup.

Jell-O Clouds

Salt Lake City, Utah

Age group: 10 to 12 months

Experienced chef: Carol Wootton

Special comments: "If you need something nutritious in a hurry, this recipe will work for you. It is also a good remedy for babies with diarrhea. This gives your baby three different textures and flavors for her palate. It can be served at any time of the day or as a snack—Jell-O is high in sugar, though, so make this a 'sometimes' food."

Prepare Jell-O according to instructions. Cool. Fold in cottage cheese and fruit before it sets.

1 box of peach-flavored Jell-O gelatin

1 cup small-curd cottage cheese

1 cup mashed bananas or pureed applesauce (use recipe in chapter 6 to make fresh)

Soup de Christophe

Sun Valley, Idaho

Age group: 10 to 12 months

Experienced chef: Ghislaine Guigon

Special comments: "This recipe has a lot of protein and vitamins; excellent for baby!"

3 carrots, peeled and finely chopped

3 potatoes, peeled

1 leek, peeled, sliced lengthwise, sand removed

1 turnip, peeled

1 cup breast milk or formula

1 egg yolk

Boil carrots, potatoes, leek, and turnip until soft. Meanwhile, mix milk or formula and yolk. Drain veggies and puree, slowly adding milk mixture. Return to saucepan, simmer for several minutes. Butter to taste.

Tip: Remember—never serve raw eggs to baby or anyone in the family—raw eggs can harbor disease-causing bacteria.

Cheese and Vegetable Chowder

Salt Lake City, Utah

Age group: 12 months and older

Experienced chef: Laurel Erickson

Special comments: "Delicious soup for the whole family!"

Cook potatoes, onions, carrots, celery, bouillon, and butter in 1 cup water for 30 minutes. In separate dish, combine flour and milk until smooth; add to vegetables. Stirring, cook until smooth and thickened. Add mustard and cheese.

1 cup diced potatoes

¾ cup chopped onions

½ cup peeled and sliced carrots

½ cup chopped celery

2 chicken bouillon cubes

⅛ cup butter

1 cup water

¼ cup all-purpose flour

1 cup breast milk or formula

½ teaspoon dry mustard

1½ cups shredded Cheddar
  cheese

Japanese Baby Rice

Salt Lake City, Utah

Age group: 12 months and older

Experienced chef: Greg Mori

Special comments: "This is a favorite Japanese baby recipe handed down through generations of Japanese families."

1 cup cooked Japanese short-grain rice (preferably Calrose brand, found in the international section of most grocery stores)

1 egg

1 teaspoon soy sauce

Prepare rice as directed. When rice is tender and water is absorbed, whip egg and soy sauce. Add to rice. Cover and continue heating for a few minutes to make sure egg heats and cooks adequately.

Tip: Remember—never serve raw eggs to baby or anyone in the family—raw eggs can harbor disease-causing bacteria.

Savory Lentils

Omaha, Nebraska

Age group: 12 months and older

Experienced chef: Tasia Koliopoulos

Special comments: "This recipe is for the baby with mature taste buds. It can be mellowed with a few minor adjustments."

Place lentils in medium saucepan, covering with 2 inches water. Bring to boil as you prepare remaining ingredients; then add to boiling lentils. Stirring occasionally, boil 30 to 40 minutes until lentils and vegetables are tender; add water as needed. (Cooking time varies, so keep watch.) Remove from heat, discard bay leaves (and garlic, if desired). Let cool slightly. Puree in food processor to desired consistency. You may keep this refrigerated for three days. Of course, if your baby has experienced allergic reactions to any of these ingredients, exclude them from the recipe and make substitutions. If your baby doesn't like strong flavors, reduce or omit garlic and bay leaf.

*You may also use split, small lentils, but if you do, cooking time may be decreased dramatically; therefore, it is very important to chop the onion, celery, and carrot extremely fine so that all ingredients will become tender at the same time.

1 cup whole lentils, rinsed
  thoroughly
1 medium onion, chopped
1 clove garlic, whole
3 bay leaves
1 celery stalk, chopped
1 large carrot, chopped
1 teaspoon tomato paste
⅓ cup olive oil

Spanakoryzo

Fort Lee, New Jersey

Age group: 12 months and older

Experienced chef: Sophia Nepolis

Special comments: "A vegetable-rice dish brimming with folic acid, a B vitamin which helps develop the child's nervous system. It's also a great side dish for adults."

¼ cup virgin olive oil

¼ cup chopped onions

1 pound spinach, washed, ends trimmed

3 cups water

1 cup uncooked short-grain white rice

1 teaspoon salt

1 teaspoon pepper

Juice of 2 lemons

½ cup chopped fresh dill

Heat oil in saucepan, add onions and spinach and sauté. When onions and spinach are limp, add 3 cups water. Heat to boiling. Add rice, salt, and pepper. Lower heat, and cook until water is absorbed, about 20 minutes. Add lemon juice and dill.

Riza Galo (Greek Rice Pudding)

Elmhurst, Illinois

Age group: 12 months and older

Experienced chef: Emila Linardakis

Special comments: "This is an excellent way to introduce some sweets to your baby while providing a nutritious dessert."

Boil water and rice. Reduce heat and simmer, stirring frequently, until all the water has been absorbed and rice is soft (about 30 minutes). Add the condensed milk, warm water, sugar, eggs, and vanilla. Stir well, cooking until thickened (about 10 to 15 minutes). Chill. Sprinkle with cinnamon.

8 cups whole milk

1 cup uncooked long-grain rice

One 15-ounce can condensed milk

1 cup warm water

2/3 cup sugar

2 eggs, well beaten

1 teaspoon vanilla

1 teaspoon ground cinnamon

Poseidon's Fish Soup

Elko, Nevada

Age group: 12 to 18 months

Experienced chef: Angelina Nepolis

Special comments: "If your child is not eating chunky food yet, you can put ingredients in a blender and puree. You can also substitute potatoes for rice."

6-ounce fish fillet, deboned
   (Dover sole or halibut)
2 carrots, peeled and chopped
2 celery stalks, chopped
1 medium tomato
1 cup uncooked white rice
2 tablespoons olive oil

Place all ingredients in pot with enough water to cover. Cook 30 to 45 minutes or until all ingredients are tender. Separate vegetables and fish from broth; mash with fork and serve to baby. Serve the remainder as a thick soup.

Morning Cereal

Virginia Beach, Virginia

Age group: 12 to 18 months

Experienced chef: Anthorla Kapos

Special comments: "The egg yolk in this recipe provides extra vitamins, protein, and flavor. You may use either milk or water, then add the baby's formula during the last simmering stage. By adding formula, you get more sweetness since formula has a sweetness of its own."

In heavy large saucepan, over medium heat, bring milk to a boil. In a small bowl, briskly stir yolk with sugar until light and fluffy. Add ½ cup hot milk to egg mixture, stirring constantly. Add any or all flavorings. Add farina to water, milk, or formula, stirring constantly. Then drizzle egg and farina mixture into milk in pan, continuing to stir. Turn heat down; simmer, stirring occasionally, until cereal thickens (about 10 minutes). If it's too hot or too thick for your baby, add a little milk.

1½ cups water, breast milk, or formula

1 egg yolk

1½ tablespoons sugar

⅛ teaspoon vanilla (optional)

Cinnamon (optional)

Orange rind (optional)

3 tablespoons farina

Vegetable Rice Soup

Salt Lake City, Utah

Age group: 13 to 18 months

Experienced chef: Pamela Kapos Zoumadakis

Special comments: "It's tasty and homemade. It gives babies something to chew, yet it's also easy to swallow."

6 cups water

4 chicken bouillon cubes

¾ cup uncooked rice

2 carrots, peeled and cut into 1-inch slices

2 celery stalks, cleaned and cut into 1-inch slices

1 tablespoon margarine

Boil 6 cups water. Add bouillon cubes, rice, carrots, and celery. Boil approximately 30 minutes, or until rice is cooked and vegetables are tender. Add margarine, stirring well. Cool slightly and serve to baby.

Tyler's Gummy Drops

Spanish Fork, Utah

Age group: 18 months and up

Experienced chef: Nancy Melander

Special comments: "This is a special sweet treat to be enjoyed once in a while, but not every day. Do not put in too much sugar—just enough to sweeten it a little."

Place juice and sugar in small saucepan and heat to boiling. Sprinkle in gelatin, and stir with wooden spoon until gelatin dissolves. Pour in pan, chill in refrigerator 1 hour. Cut into cubes.

Tip: If desired, you can use your child's favorite juice or any combination of juices.

1/4 cup each: apple juice, orange juice, pineapple juice, cranberry juice cocktail

1/4 teaspoon sugar

1 envelope unflavored gelatin

CHAPTER 9

Recipes for a Toddler's Family

I do not like broccoli. And I haven't liked it since I was a little kid and my mother made me eat it. And I'm president of the United States, and I'm not going to eat any more broccoli.
—George Bush, president of the United States, 1988–1992

Once your infant is one year old, we give him a new title: "toddler." Toddlers can begin adapting their taste buds to ethnic foods and spices. This is a good age for introducing more diverse flavors and preparing your child for unfamiliar tastes—the age where feeding your toddler "junk food" is sometimes easier. Try some favorites for children, which are recipes for dishes the entire family can eat. The following international recipes are suitable for toddlers.

Flavors from China

Egg Drop Soup with Rice

Primary nutrients: B vitamins, protein

Stir broth and rice together in saucepan, bringing to a boil. Add eggs and continue to stir. Add lemon juice and pepper as desired.

Serves 4

4 cups chicken broth

1 cup cooked rice

2 eggs (both whites and yolks), beaten

Lemon juice

Pepper

Sweet and Sour Chicken

Primary nutrient: Iron

Serves 4

4 boneless chicken breasts

Salt

Pepper

2 tablespoons vegetable oil

1 onion, peeled and sliced

4 ounces carrots, peeled and
sliced

One 7-ounce can pineapple
chunks, drained

2 tablespoons wine vinegar

2 level tablespoons brown sugar

1 tablespoon lemon juice

2 level teaspoons tomato paste

½ teaspoon Worcestershire
sauce

1 red bell pepper, sliced and
seeded

1 green bell pepper, sliced and
seeded

2 level teaspoons cornstarch

1 to 2 tablespoons cold water

Preheat oven to 375 degrees Fahrenheit. Trim chicken, and season lightly with salt and pepper. Heat oil in pan, and brown chicken. Transfer to casserole dish. Fry onion and carrots in the same oil 2 to 3 minutes. Combine pineapple with vinegar, brown sugar, lemon juice, tomato paste, and Worcestershire sauce. Add to pan, and bring to boil. Arrange bell pepper pieces over chicken, and pour half the sauce over all. Bake, covered, 45 minutes or until chicken is tender. Blend cornstarch with 1 to 2 tablespoons cold water until smooth, and add to remaining sauce. Bring sauce to boil, and cook until thickened. Pour remaining sauce over chicken right before serving.

Recipes from America

Whole Wheat Waffles

Primary nutrients: B vitamins, calcium, protein

Preheat waffle iron. Sift together flours, baking powder, and sugar. With mixer, blend eggs, milk, and oil. Add flour mixture; stir just until blended (do not over-mix). Spread batter on iron; cook until golden brown. Serve with applesauce or top with vanilla yogurt and sliced fruit.

Serves 4

¾ cup all-purpose flour

¾ cup whole wheat flour

4 teaspoons baking powder

2 tablespoons sugar

2 eggs

1 cup low-fat milk

2 tablespoons vegetable oil

Banana French Toast

Primary nutrients: B vitamins, protein

Beat banana and eggs together with electric mixer. Stir in milk and nutmeg. Heat butter in small skillet. Dip bread in banana mixture; place in hot skillet. Cook until browned on both sides.

Serves 6

1 medium banana

2 eggs

⅓ cup low-fat milk

⅛ teaspoon nutmeg

1 tablespoon butter

6 slices whole wheat bread

Banana Porridge

Primary nutrient: Potassium

Serves 2

1 banana

⅛ teaspoon salt

⅓ cup rolled oats

¾ cup water

Cut banana into small pieces. Place in small saucepan, and add remaining ingredients. Bring to boil, stirring constantly. Cook 8 minutes. Remove from heat. Let stand 5 minutes before serving.

Peach-Maple Waffle Syrup

Primary nutrient: Vitamin C

Serves 4

1¾ cups chopped peaches

⅓ cup maple syrup

Puree peaches in blender. Place in saucepan. Stir in syrup. Simmer 5 minutes over low heat. Use to top waffles or French toast.

Strawberry-Maple Syrup

Primary nutrient: Vitamin C

1¾ cups chopped strawberries

⅓ cup maple syrup

Puree strawberries in blender. Place in saucepan. Stir in syrup. Simmer 5 minutes over low heat. Use to top waffles or French toast.

Banana Prune Bread

Primary nutrients: Potassium, B vitamins

Preheat oven to 350 degrees Fahrenheit. Grease loaf pan with cooking oil spray. In large bowl, mix dry ingredients. Use an electric mixer to thoroughly combine bananas, prunes, brown sugar, lemon, egg substitute, and vanilla. Add to dry ingredients. Mix just until moistened. Pour batter into loaf pan. Bake 45 to 50 minutes, or until knife inserted in center comes out clean. Let cool 10 minutes in pan, then cool completely on rack.

Tip: Small (4-ounce) jars of baby food prunes, applesauce, or other fruits substitute for part of the oil in baked goods. Prunes carry the flavor of chocolate well, while applesauce works great in most cakes and cookies. Typically you can substitute fruit puree for half of the oil in a recipe.

Makes 1 loaf

2 cups all-purpose flour

1/2 teaspoon salt

1/4 teaspoon baking soda

1/2 tablespoon baking powder

1 teaspoon cinnamon

Dash of allspice

4 ripe bananas, mashed

2 jars baby-food prunes (or use fresh pureed prunes)

1/2 cup packed brown sugar

Juice of one lemon

Zest of half a lemon

4 tablespoons egg substitute, beaten

1 1/2 teaspoons vanilla

Apple Pudding

Primary nutrients: Vitamin C, calcium, B vitamins

Mix rice and applesauce together in large bowl. Add yogurt and cinnamon. Stir well. Spoon into dishes and serve.

Serves 4

1 cup cooked rice

1 cup applesauce

1 cup low-fat vanilla yogurt

1 teaspoon cinnamon

Baked Apple

Primary nutrient: Vitamin C

Serves 1

1 cooking apple

1 teaspoon honey

1 tablespoon orange juice

1 to 2 teaspoons of walnuts, chopped

Wash apple. Remove core with an apple corer, keeping apple whole. Place on plate or small microwave-safe baking dish. Drizzle honey, juice, and nuts in center and over top. Bake in microwave on high 3 to 5 minutes or until tender. (Allow additional time for more than one apple.) You may also add enough water to cover the bottom of the baking dish and bake in a regular oven 10 to 15 minutes at 400 degrees Fahrenheit. For variety, try using brown sugar, a dot of margarine, a sprinkle of cinnamon, and several raisins in the apple center.

Fruit Juice Pops

Primary nutrient: Vitamin C

Serves 6

6-ounce can frozen juice concentrate (100% juice)

2 cups plain yogurt

2 teaspoons vanilla

Six 5-ounce paper cups

6 wooden craft (Popsicle) sticks or plastic spoons

Mix all ingredients together in medium bowl and blend until smooth. Pour mixture into paper cups (generous ⅓ cup mixture per cup). Insert one stick or plastic spoon in each. Cover with wax paper, and freeze until firm.

Note: To remove a juice pop, hold the paper cup under tap water for a few seconds.

Tastes of India

Curried Chicken

Primary nutrients: Protein and iron

Preheat oven to 375 degrees Fahrenheit. Heat oil in oven-safe heavy saucepan. Add garlic, ginger, and chicken; sauté over medium heat, turning to brown chicken evenly. Add curry, bay leaves, cumin, and coriander. Sauté and stir 1 minute. Add onion, celery, carrot, tomato, tomato paste, lemon juice, and broth; bring mixture to boil. Bake in oven, covered, 30 minutes, turning chicken pieces occasionally. Serve with warmed rice. Salt and pepper to taste if needed.

Serves 4

3 tablespoons vegetable oil

2 teaspoons chopped garlic

2 teaspoons chopped fresh ginger

4 boneless chicken breasts

2 tablespoons curry powder

2 bay leaves

1 tablespoon ground cumin

1 teaspoon ground coriander

½ cup chopped onion

½ cup chopped celery

½ cup peeled, chopped carrot

1 small tomato, chopped

2 tablespoons tomato paste

2 tablespoons fresh lemon juice

1 cup chicken stock or canned broth

Salt

Pepper

2 cups cooked white rice

Flavors from Italy

Spaghetti with Mozzarella Meatballs

Primary nutrients: Iron, B vitamins, protein

Serves 4

1 pound lean ground beef

1 cup bread crumbs

1 clove garlic, chopped

26 tablespoons parsley,
   chopped and separated

Salt

Pepper

1 egg, beaten

5 ounces mozzarella

1 tablespoon vegetable oil

1 onion, chopped

2 medium tomatoes, chopped

12 ounces uncooked spaghetti

4 tablespoons fresh parsley,
   chopped

Mix beef, bread crumbs, garlic, half the parsley, salt, and pepper in a bowl. Add egg, and mix well. Cut cheese into 1-inch cubes. Take about a tablespoon of the beef mixture and form into a ball around each cube of cheese. Heat oil in large pan. Add meatballs and brown, turning occasionally. Add onion and then tomatoes (with juice). Simmer, covered, 30 minutes. Separately cook spaghetti according to package directions. Drain. Serve meatballs over top of spaghetti. Sprinkle with parsley.

Tastes of Greece

Spanakopita

Primary nutrients: Iron, folate, B vitamins, protein

Preheat oven to 400 degrees Fahrenheit. Boil or steam spinach 3 to 5 minutes. Drain. In a large skillet, sauté onions in olive oil over medium heat until tender, stirring constantly. Add spinach, water, seasonings, and herbs and cook until liquid is absorbed. Sprinkle Cream of Wheat over the top of the mixture and cool. In a large bowl, combine eggs and cheeses. Stir in spinach mixture, blending well. Set aside. Remove phyllo from package and lay out on dry surface. Cover with slightly damp clean dishtowel, as the phyllo will dry out and crumble quickly. Brush baking pan with butter. Line pan with three sheets of phyllo. Spread enough cheese mixture to lightly cover phyllo. Layer with three more sheets of phyllo. Spread with cheese mixture. Repeat until pie is 2 inches thick. Top with phyllo, and brush again with butter. Bake 20 minutes or until golden brown and crisp.

Tip: In a hurry? Use one 10-ounce package of frozen spinach, thawed and drained, instead of fresh spinach.

Serves 12

3 packages (10 ounces each) fresh spinach, washed and coarsely chopped

3 green onions, finely chopped

¼ cup olive oil

¼ cup water

1 teaspoon salt

¼ cup minced fresh dill

¼ cup minced fresh mint

¼ cup minced fresh parsley

1 teaspoon Cream of Wheat

5 eggs

1 cup cottage cheese

1½ cups crumbled feta cheese

One 1-pound package phyllo dough

1 to 1¼ cups melted butter

Dolmathes (Stuffed Grape Leaves)

Primary nutrients: Protein, beta-carotene

Serves 8

1 pound lean ground beef

1 medium onion, peeled and
    chopped

15-ounce can whole tomatoes
    (or 3 medium fresh,
    chopped)

1 teaspoon salt

½ teaspoon pepper

½ teaspoon garlic powder

1 teaspoon fresh chopped
    parsley, mint, fennel, or dill

½ cup uncooked short-grain
    rice

1 pound grape leaves (sold in
    most Mediterranean specialty
    stores)

2 lemons, juiced

1½ cups canned beef broth

Mix beef, onion, tomatoes, salt, pepper, garlic, and herbs. Blend rice into mixture. Rinse grape leaves in cold water; drain. Cut off stems. Roll 1 table-spoon mixture in each leaf. Layer in saucepan, squeezing lemon juice over each layer; pour beef broth over all. Simmer, covered, 1 hour and 15 minutes or until rice is tender. For ten-to-twelve-month-olds, puree cooked rolls.

Flavors from Mexico

Chicken Enchiladas

Primary nutrient: Iron

Preheat oven to 350 degrees Fahrenheit. Lightly oil a 13 × 9 baking pan. Puree tomatoes (you should be good at this by now!), onion, garlic, and chilies in blender. Heat ¼ cup of oil in saucepan, and cook tomato mixture 8 minutes. Heat remaining oil in small frying pan. Fry tortillas on both sides, one at a time; remove from pan, keeping them stacked and warm. Dip each tortilla in sauce to coat lightly. Add a little chicken. Place tortillas, rolled seam down, in baking dish. Pour the remaining sauce over all. Cover baking dish with foil and bake 30 minutes. Remove foil; spread cream over the top of the enchiladas. Top with cheese.

Tip: To control the heat, remove seeds from chilies (use gloves to handle, or place your hands in plastic bags then throw away). Be sure to wash hands before touching baby, as the oils from the chilies can burn.

Serves 4

1¼ pounds ripe tomatoes

1 medium onion, peeled and chopped

1 clove garlic, chopped

4 to 6 serrano chilies

½ cup vegetable oil

32 corn tortillas

3 chicken breast halves, cut into small pieces

1 cup heavy cream

1 pound Cheddar cheese, grated

Tastes of Scotland

Barley Broth

Primary nutrients: B vitamins

Serves 8

1 onion, diced

1 leek, thoroughly washed and thinly sliced

2 carrots, peeled and diced

2 tablespoons butter

2 cups diced turnips

8 cups vegetable stock (Make your own by putting broccoli, celery, carrots, and leeks in boiling water and cooking 20 minutes.)

1 teaspoon yeast extract (or soy sauce, if you can't find)

¼ cup barley bran (sold at natural food stores)

1 cup brussels sprouts, shredded

Place onion, leek, carrots, and butter in a large, heavy-based frying pan. Sauté 3 minutes at medium heat. Add turnips, stock, yeast, and barley; bring to boil. Simmer 30 minutes. Add brussels sprouts; simmer 2 minutes.

CHAPTER 10

Recipes for Restlessness and Allergies

by Dr. Alexander Golbin

Our lives are not in the lap of the gods, but in the lap of our cooks.
—Lin Yutang, "On Food and Medicine," *The Importance of Living*

A s I've discussed throughout this book, some things to look for as you experiment with and introduce foods to your baby are allergies and sleeplessness. These conditions occur frequently, but I've provided some recipes that may help the problems.

Restful Recipes

How does food make a baby sleep? In general, foods containing carbohydrates and a certain type of protein (an amino acid called tryptophan) will help to produce a chemical in the brain that allows a person to focus, feel calm, and eventually fall asleep. B vitamins help support the nervous system in general, and some of them help in the production of serotonin, the sleep-inducing brain chemical. The mineral magnesium also supports the production of serotonin.

Note: Do not try to increase serotonin levels in children with asthma, as high serotonin levels constrict the airways of asthmatics.

Keep the diet balanced. A healthy, balanced diet of whole, unprocessed foods is the best "medicine" for any child. But if there are times when you feel your toddler might need a little help to settle down and/or sleep, try some of the following recipes rich in protein, carbohydrates, B vitamins, and magnesium. These recipes are only for children who can eat and chew well, those around three years old.

Sleep Tight Tuna Sandwiches

Primary nutrients: Protein, carbohydrate, magnesium, B vitamins

⅓ cup water-packed tuna, drained and flaked

2 slices whole wheat bread

2 tablespoons ground sesame seeds

2 ounces Monterey Jack cheese (the equivalent of one slice)

Arrange tuna on one slice of bread. Sprinkle with sesame seeds. Cover with cheese. Place under broiler for several minutes until cheese melts. Top with remaining slice of bread. Cut sandwich in half and serve.

Lullaby Baked Apple

Primary nutrients: Magnesium, calcium, carbohydrates

Slice apple half into several slices and place in small baking dish coated with vegetable cooking spray. Top with raisins, walnuts, and cheese. Cover and bake at 375 degrees Fahrenheit for 15 minutes.

½ red apple
Vegetable cooking spray
¼ cup raisins
¼ cup walnuts, ground
½ cup shredded Cheddar cheese

Popeye Popcorn Snacks

Primary nutrients: Magnesium, carbohydrates

Mix Parmesan, Cheddar, peanuts, and sunflower seeds. Toss with hot popcorn.

2 teaspoons Parmesan cheese
2 tablespoons shredded Cheddar cheese
2 tablespoons peanuts
3 tablespoons sunflower seeds
1 cup popcorn (unsalted)

Easy Stuffed Celery

Make sure your child can chew well before you serve her celery. If you are unsure, save this recipe until she is older.

Primary nutrients: B vitamins, protein, magnesium

¼ cup peanut butter

1 teaspoon honey

1 tablespoon sunflower seeds

1 celery stalk

Mix peanut butter with honey. Add sunflower seeds. Spread on celery.

Easy Cheese Snacks

Primary nutrients: B vitamins, protein, calcium, magnesium

1 date

Two 1-inch cubes Cheddar
  cheese

2 walnut halves

Place date in the middle of toothpick. Add a cheese cube at each end. Add walnut halves and serve.

Note: Make sure children understand that toothpicks are not toys!

Variation: Use apple slice in middle instead of date.

Peanut Butter Shake

Primary nutrients: B vitamins, protein, calcium, magnesium, potassium

Blend all in food processor. Serve creamy.
    Variation: Add a sprinkle of cinnamon.

- ¼ cup peanut butter
- ¾ cup milk
- 6 cubes frozen milk (to make, freeze whole milk in an ice cube tray)
- 1 frozen banana
- 1 tablespoon protein powder (purchase at a natural-food store)
- 1 tablespoon honey

Banana Sandwich

Primary nutrients: B vitamins, protein, magnesium

Stir protein powder into peanut butter. Spread on bread. Top with banana slices. Serve with milk.

- ½ tablespoon protein powder
- 3 tablespoons peanut butter
- 1 slice whole wheat bread
- 1 banana

Potato Snacks

Primary nutrients: B vitamins, calcium, magnesium, protein, carbohydrates

2 teaspoons Parmesan cheese
¾ cup shredded Cheddar cheese
3 tablespoons ground sunflower
  seeds
1 baked potato

Mix cheeses, and add seeds. Stuff mixture into potato, or cut potato into slices and serve mixture on top of slices. Broil 5 minutes in oven.

Recipes for the Allergic Child

Some children have allergic responses to certain foods, which they often outgrow, but can retain for a lifetime. This section alerts you to potential allergy-causing foods.

What's the deal with allergies? The word allergy is derived from the Greek words "allos" meaning "altered" and "ergan" meaning "work" or "action." A food allergy causes an "altered action," such as a rash, headache, or nasal congestion to take place in the body. An allergic response typically happens when a large, partially digested protein molecule is absorbed. The body thinks this is a foreign, invading substance so it produces antibodies to fight off the foreign antigen. The production of antibodies causes the symptoms typically associated with allergies.

Recipes with Carob

Carob, which you can find in the baking section of your favorite natural-food store, is a great substitute for chocolate. It has a dif-

Most Common Allergenic Foods

Cow's milk	Corn	Wheat
Soy	Chocolate	Egg whites
Nuts (especially peanuts)	Seafood	Citrus
Yeast	Red and yellow dyes	

Least Allergenic Foods

Rice	Sweet potatoes	Grapes
Lettuce	Oats	Applesauce
Barley	Carrots	Squash

ferent flavor than chocolate, but still makes rich, tasty desserts. Carob is made from ground pods of the honey locust tree. Unlike chocolate, it does not contain caffeine. Start children out with carob, rather than chocolate, for that occasional treat.

Carob Milk

Primary nutrients: Protein, carbohydrate, calcium, vitamin D

Blend all ingredients and serve.

1 cup milk

1 tablespoon carob chips, melted

2 teaspoons honey

Carob Banana Cookies

Primary nutrients: Protein, carbohydrate, and fiber

1 egg

¼ cup apple juice

¼ cup vegetable oil

¼ cup wheat germ

¾ cup carob chips

1 cup oats

¼ cup mashed banana

Preheat oven to 350 degrees Fahrenheit. Beat egg and apple juice together. Mix in oil, wheat germ, carob, and oats. Mix in banana. Drop by spoonfuls onto nonstick baking sheet. Bake 10 minutes. Cool on rack.

Carob Banana Brownies

Primary nutrients: Protein, carbohydrate, calcium, fiber

2 eggs

½ cup mashed banana

⅓ cup vegetable oil

1 teaspoon vanilla extract

1 cup milk

¼ cup whole wheat flour

2 tablespoons wheat germ

¼ cup carob powder

¼ teaspoon baking soda

2 cups oats

Preheat oven to 350 degrees Fahrenheit. Beat eggs, banana, oil, vanilla extract, and milk until creamy. Mix in remaining ingredients. Bake 10 minutes on nonstick baking sheet.

Recipes with Honey

Honey is considered a natural source of sugar. It is a little easier for baby's body to metabolize than refined white sugar because it is composed of 75 percent sucrose and 25 percent fructose. Fructose does not require insulin to be metabolized, so it might not affect baby's blood sugar levels as much as table sugar. You should never give honey to a child under one year of age, however, because honey contains the risk of a bacterium known as *Clostridium botulinum,* which can cause severe food poisoning in a young child. Honey is safe for children over the age of one.

Honey Cookies

Primary nutrients: Carbohydrate, fiber

Preheat oven to 375 degrees Fahrenheit. Mix honey and oil with flour, baking soda, baking powder, and salt. Add vanilla. Drop by spoonfuls on greased baking sheet. Bake 15 minutes.

½ cup honey

⅓ cup vegetable oil

1 cup barley flour

¼ teaspoon baking soda

½ teaspoon baking powder

¼ teaspoon salt

½ teaspoon vanilla extract

Honey Butter

Primary nutrients: Carbohydrate, fat

Mix honey and butter. It's a great topping for pancakes, waffles, or French toast. Refrigerate after use.

½ cup honey

½ cup butter, softened

Honey–Peanut Butter Yogurt

Primary nutrients: Protein, calcium

4 tablespoons honey

1 teaspoon butter

½ cup peanut butter

1 cup plain yogurt

Bring honey and butter to a boil. Remove from heat and add peanut butter. Allow to cool slightly. Use as a topping with yogurt.

Foods to Avoid on a Wheat-Free Diet

Most bread, including multigrain breads

Wheat germ

Enriched flour

Farina

Durham flour

Pancakes

Bread crumbs

Ovaltine

Graham flour

Wheat bran

Wheat starch

Gluten

Doughnuts

Most pastas, such as spaghetti and noodles

Desserts made with flour

Graham crackers

Malt

Processed foods with hydrolyzed vegetable protein, modified food starch, vegetables starches, vegetable gums

Determining allergic foods. If you suspect your child might be allergic to a particular food, discuss it with your pediatrician,

Milk Allergies

The University of Brussels in Belgium studied thirty-three infants who had difficulty falling asleep (and staying asleep) and found that almost all had an allergy to milk. After milk was eliminated from their diets, their sleep improved. When they again received milk, insomnia returned. But parents should not jump to conclusions. In reality, an allergy to milk is not common. If your child does end up being allergic to milk or having a lactose intolerance that prevents him from digesting milk, it is vitally important that you give your child calcium from other sources. Calcium is necessary to build the bones your child will depend on for a lifetime. Consult your pediatrician or a dietitian to find out how to make sure your child can get adequate calcium without dairy foods.

who can instruct you on how to keep track of food intake and occurrence of symptoms.

The allergy test. He or she may have you try what's known as an "elimination diet," in which you eliminate the suspect food for a while then serve it several days later and watch for allergic symptoms. For example, if you suspect your child is allergic to wheat, serve her other grains instead of wheat for five days. Read the labels on everything you are preparing to ensure that no wheat products are present. On the sixth day, serve your child wheat, such as a piece of wheat bread. Watch for a reaction in the next hour. If no reaction occurs, give some additional wheat. Watch for a reaction during the remainder of the day and for twenty-four hours afterward.

Milk-Containing Foods

All milk (chocolate, half and half, evaporated,1%, 2%, skim, buttermilk, and milk solids)

Cheese

Creamed soups

Mashed potatoes (due to milk/butter)

Creamy salad dressing

Milk chocolate

Many baked goods

Many baking mixes

Butter

Yogurt

Custard

Cream, sour cream (including imitation), whipping cream, and buttermilk

Desserts made with milk (pudding, ice cream, some sherbets, for example)

Processed foods with whey, curds, casein, caseinate, sodium caseinate, lactalbumin

Foods to Avoid on an Egg-Free Diet

If your child is allergic to eggs, you will need to avoid these foods:

Pancakes

Breads and baked goods made with egg

Egg dishes

Meringues

Marshmallow products

Many batter-dipped foods

Boiled frostings

Processed foods with albumin, egg white solids, egg yolks

Noodles

Mayonnaise

Cake mixes with eggs

Macaroons

Fondants and other candies

Tartar sauce

Beverages such as eggnog and shakes

CHAPTER 11

Making Seasonal, Holiday, and Birthday Foods Fun

To be happy at home is the ultimate result of all ambition.
—Samuel Johnson

Different seasons bring changes in the climate and distinctive holidays to celebrate. And, of course, there's that one extra special day each year—your child's birthday. Serving foods and planning activities that fit the weather or reinforce a seasonal theme can greatly enhance special occasions for your child. Many of the treats in this chapter contain sugar. Sugar is full of waistline-expanding calories but offers no vitamins or minerals for your growing child. Sugar can also cause dental cavities, and many parents feel that it adversely affects their child's behavior. It's a good idea to limit the amount of sugar your child has on a daily basis so as not to develop a strong sweet tooth. Serve sugary seasonal treats only occasionally. You might find it helpful to base as many treats as possible on fruits—they're naturally sweet and are packed full of nutrients that growing bodies need. This chapter includes party ideas and activities for your baby (soon to be toddler). I've provided ideas that take you up to age 3.

Parties for Birthdays and Other Occasions

Baby Food Pure and Simple isn't all work and no play. I have put together some party ideas and recipes, starting with your child's first birthday. Bear in mind that this party is really for the adults. The baby has usually smeared cake all over his or her face, and the camera is the most important object to have at the party. Involve family members such as grandparents, godparents, neighbors, aunts, and uncles. Keep necessities handy for parents with children, including these:

Disposable diapers

Baby wipes

Coloring books and crayons for older children

Camera with extra film

First Birthday

The first birthday is the most special, so put some time into the cake (though most of it will be thrown on the floor).

First Birthday Cake

Preheat oven to 350 degrees Fahrenheit. Grease and flour two 9-inch cake pans. Cream together butter and honey. Add eggs and mix. In separate bowl mix dry ingredients. Fold in sour cream. Mix the flour mixture with honey/butter mixture. Pour into pans. Bake 40 minutes. Frost with Honey–Peanut Butter Icing (see below).

1 cup butter

1½ cups honey

4 eggs, beaten

2 cups sifted unbleached white flour

2 teaspoons baking soda

1 teaspoon ground cinnamon

1 teaspoon ground ginger

¼ teaspoon salt

1⅓ cups sour cream

Honey–Peanut Butter Icing

Mix butter and honey in saucepan and bring to boil. Remove from heat and add peanut butter. Mix well. Spread over your baby's First Birthday Cake.

4 tablespoons butter

¼ cup honey

½ cup peanut butter

Ages Two to Three

Now you're entering into the wonderland of traditional birthday parties. By age two, most children are pretty excited about parties, colors, and gifts. They still are not ready for elaborate preparations, however. Themes are useful when planning your child's party. Organizing a party around a theme fosters fun and creativity for the host and the guests. Keep themes simple, with bright colors and fun sounds. An adult should accompany each

> ## Birthday Food Ideas
>
> Birthday cake with candles (or cupcakes)
>
> Fresh fruit slices with vanilla yogurt for dip
>
> Low-sugar cereal mix, colorfully decorated
>
> Teething biscuits

child of this age attending the party.

Time to allow: One-and-a-half hours.

Here are some suggestions for these ages.

Color Party

Ask your party goers to wear the color of your little one's choice, and decorate with the same color (tablecloth and plates, frosting on cake, candles, and so on). Kids can Velcro the tail on the same color donkey, and you can help them play a game where everyone thinks of things that are the same color.

Alphabet Party

Decorate your table with letters of the alphabet; get white butcher paper to use for a tablecloth. Set out crayons and washable marker (the smelly kind that are not toxic). Kids will enjoy scribbling on the butcher paper. Use colored letters as festive pin-ups.

Stuffed Animal Party

Ask each guest to bring his or her favorite stuffed animal, and allow place settings for furry friends. Read stories about Winnie-the-Pooh or from other favorite books.

Dino or Barney Party

Everything can reflect the theme name: invitations, cake, or cupcakes decorated with tiny Dino/Barneys. If you have a sandbox, this is the perfect time to go on a sandbox dig for dino bones (you can bury tiny plastic dinosaurs or other favors).

Story Party

Ask each guest to bring a favorite book, then sit in a circle and share. You or another parent can be the designated reader. When story time is over, let your guests color and decorate their own "books" with crayons and stickers. (Provide small, blank-page books you have hole-punched and tied together in advance.) Decorate your home with storybooks, and/or ask your guests to come dressed as their favorite storybook characters (parents can help with costumes).

Magic Party

Kids love magic, and a magic-theme birthday party can be a real hit.

Magic Party Activities

Hire a magician to entertain.

Teach the children simple magic tricks.

Create magic carpets. Give each child a piece of yellow poster board. Get glue, scissors, cardboard paper, fabric, and other decorating goodies. Have each child decorate his or her own magic carpet. If the magic carpets have time to dry, you might even have a magic carpet race (outdoors would work best for this).

Restless Rabbits. This is a fun game also known as Sardines, because the kids end up packed together. This game is the opposite of hide-and-seek: One player hides, and the other players hunt for the hidden player. When a player finds the hiding place, silently that player hides, too. As each hunter discovers the hiding spot, he or she also hides in the same spot. The game continues until the last player (called the magician) finds the restless rabbits.

Fun foods. There are several "magical food items" that you can serve. The trick is finding a mystical angle for typical party food items. For example:

• *Secret Sandwiches.* Cut peanut butter and jelly sandwiches into different shapes, such as wands, hats, or rabbit ears.

• *Pretty Fruit.* Prepare a watermelon fruit basket by cutting out different kinds of fruit in the shapes of stars, wands, bunnies, and moons.

Ten Planning Ideas for Successful Parties

• *Plan your party:* A good party needs planning. If you are especially busy, it may take up to six weeks to accomplish everything at a comfortable pace. Plan the party with your child. Keep realistic expectations. Select fun invitations, and send them out about two weeks ahead of time.

• *Select appropriate activities:* Most young children enjoy what they know best: cakes, songs, balloons, and games.

• *Invite the right number of guests:* Allow your child to participate in this part of the planning. Talk to your child to make sure his or her special friends are included on the invitation list.

• *Keep decorations fun and simple:* You can usually find patterns that feature the latest popular characters. Using plates, napkins, cups, and favors that match makes a fun theme. Don't forget the balloons and streamers in coordinating colors! Music related to the themes will also get the children in the mood.

• *Provide party favors:* Think of unusual party favors that relate to your theme. The favors kids make themselves will be especially memorable. Painted T-shirts, hats, headbands, or frames including Polaroid pictures can be fun.

• *Limit party time:* Be specific about when the party starts and ends. Keep it small, simple, and short, especially for children under three years old.

• *Honor the birthday child:* Work to make the birthday boy or girl feel special at the party. Create a birthday seat at the table or in the party room. Make sure the birthday child is "it" or goes first in the games.

• *Keep the party atmosphere positive:* Don't let little mishaps ruin the party. Be prepared before the party starts for spills and keep all breakable items out of the party room. Keep the atmosphere positive.

• *Choose age-appropriate activities and games:* Start with crafts or activities that involve the children as they arrive. Once all guests have arrived, have one craft and two to three games planned, depending on the ages. Plan more games than you may need so you can move on if a game isn't working. Make sure everyone feels good by playing noncompetitive games. Have cool-down activities toward the end of the party. For example, have children sit down and watch a video.

• *Serve foods that kids like:* Kids love birthday cake and ice cream! Other foods can be simple, such as frozen yogurt or fruit juice pops. But never overlook the corner bakery; they may have some terrific suggestions.

Ten Party Pitfalls

- *Inviting too many kids.* An overly enthusiastic parent invites too many kids.

- *Inviting the wrong mix of kids.* Even the most cautious parent can sabotage their child's party by inviting the wrong mix of kids. Invite guests within an age range of one to two years.

- *Allowing unexpected guests to attend.* Ask parents to keep guest list to invitees only.

- *Providing insufficient supervision.* Prepare by asking a couple of relatives to help.

- *Throwing the party during nap time.* Children become grumpy. Avoid throwing parties during nap times.

- *Planning too many activities.* Bingo, pin the tail on the donkey, pizza making, cupcake baking, and party hat crafting are all loads of fun—but result in chaos if not limited to what you can tackle. As a rule of thumb, two to three activities should work out fine.

- *Forgetting to set boundaries.* Set boundaries at the outset of your party, announcing that "Today our party zone is right here in the fun room" or "This

Parties for Season Reasons

As the seasons change, so do children's moods. Springtime is alive with flowers and the children are restless to go outside and enjoy the new sunshine. Summertime is an invitation to swim fenced-in area is our official fun zone!" Tell guests exactly what to expect. "First we will play three party games. Then *everyone* gets a prize."

- *Serving too much sugar and too little nutrition.* Yes, cake and ice cream are expected at birthday parties. Balance sweets by stuffing goody bags with packets of pretzels, raisins, or rice cakes. Serve unsweetened beverages or low-fat milk. Provide healthful snacks such as fresh fruit, vegetable kabobs, baked tortilla chips with salsa, air-popped popcorn, or low-fat trail mix.

- *Letting gift-opening turn into chaos.* Kids can be territorial and your gift-exchange can create commotion. Sometimes it's best to wait to unwrap gifts after the party. If that's the case, snap a photo of your child unwrapping each gift, and slip the appropriate photo into each thank-you note. If you opt to open gifts at the party, wait until near the end to begin the unwrapping process. By opening gifts beforehand, children may want to play with the gifts and start fighting over them.

- *Forgetting the party's purpose.* Well-meaning parents forget the ultimate purpose of a party is for kids to have fun! Keep that idea in mind, and your child's next birthday party is bound to be a blue-ribbon event!

and cool off—and to have fun in the sun. Fall is the season that gets kids excited for the holidays, but may also make them feel a little confined since they can't play outside in the lovely weather. And winter is the cozy time—but also a boring time—for children who are ready for spring.

Festive Ideas for Springtime

Spring is a time of great joy. Flowers begin to blossom, and Easter is a great holiday for both special foods and special activities. Eggs symbolize Easter, as do Easter bunnies. Both have their origins in pre-Christian celebrations of spring and renewal. Easter egg hunts, indoors or out, can be exciting events for children. Prepare ahead for springtime neighborhood gatherings that your children will remember.

Neighborhood Egg-Dip Party

Age: 2 to 3

Invite each child to bring six hard-boiled eggs. Furnish materials for dyeing (food coloring, and so on) and trimming (paper, lace, buttons, ribbons, and feathers). Give each child a basket in which to carry home the decorated eggs. Serve the Easter Bunny helpers Basket Cupcakes with Bunny Sandwiches and milk!

Bunny Sandwich

Age: 2 to 3

Loaf of white bread, sliced
Butter, softened
Ham slices
Lettuce
Carrot

Cut slices of bread with bunny cookie cutter. Spread with butter. Fill with sliced ham and lettuce trimmed to fit. Add a bit of carrot for bunny's eyes; place a slice of carrot in bunny's paw.

Basket Cupcakes

Age: 2 to 3

Make cake mix, substituting applesauce for oil and use egg whites or egg substitute instead of whole eggs. Bake as directed in muffin pan using paper liners. Place flaked coconut in small bowl. Sprinkle with several drops of green food coloring. Work coloring into coconut with your fingers, adding more coloring until you reach desired color. Frost cupcakes. Decorate frosted cupcakes with green tinted coconut. Push jelly beans into frosting to represent "eggs," then bend a licorice stick and push ends into frosting to form a handle for a springtime basket. Make sure your licorice stick is not too stiff so it will bend easily and stick to the frosting.

1 cake mix, any flavor

One 4-ounce jar baby food applesauce

Eggs or egg substitute, as directed on cake mix package

1 cup sweetened, flaked coconut

Green food coloring

1 package reduced-fat white frosting

Candy: jelly beans and thin licorice

Pear Bunnies

Age: 1 to 2

Canned pears make great bunny bodies! Drain pears. Lay ½ canned pear on a bed of lettuce. Add green food coloring to cottage cheese and stir. Arrange green cottage cheese around base of pear to resemble grass. Use cheese sticks for ears, raisins for eyes and nose.

1 large can of pears, in "lite" syrup or pear juice concentrate

4 large lettuce leaves

1 cup 2% cottage cheese

Green food coloring

8 small cheese sticks

12 raisins

Festive Ideas for Summertime

During the hot summer months, appetites tend to shrink. Summer fun and heat also mean that little ones are thirsty and can easily get dehydrated. Ices, ice pops, and popsicles are popular during this time of the year. Here are some ideas for nutritious, tempting meals and snacks.

Hobo Dinner

Independence Day is a great holiday for creating themes. The Baby Gourmet recommends this Hobo Dinner for camping or after hiking.

Age: 2 to 3

1 pound ground beef
Shortening (for greasing)
Four 1-pound coffee cans
4 tomatoes, sliced
17-ounce can whole kernel
   corn, drained
Salt
Pepper
Butter
1 cup Bisquick baking mix
1/3 cup milk

Shape beef into four patties; place one patty in each of four lightly greased 1-pound coffee cans. Top each patty with three tomato slices and ¼ of the corn. Season with salt and pepper; dot with butter. Cover each can with heavy-duty aluminum foil. Place cans on grill 3 to 4 inches from coals; cook 20 to 30 minutes. Meanwhile, stir baking mix and milk to form soft dough; drop 3 spoonfuls into each can. Cook, uncovered, 10 minutes longer.

Ices

Make a base syrup by combining the 2 cups water and 2 cups sugar. Cook on low boil 7 to 10 minutes, then use flavorings below to make tasty, refreshing ices.

Basic Ingredients:
2 cups water
2 cups sugar

Variations:

Grape Ice: 2 cups 100% grape juice, $2/3$ cup 100% orange juice, 3 tablespoons lemon juice

Lemon Ice: $3/4$ cup lemon juice squeezed from fresh lemons, 2 cups water

Orange Ice: 2 cups 100% orange juice, $1/4$ cup lemon juice

Apple Ice: 2 cups 100% apple juice, 3 tablespoons lemon juice

Pour into small bowl and freeze until mushy (approximately 1 hour). Stir, then pour into ice pop (Popsicle) trays; freeze until firm, approximately 2 hours.

Orangesicles

Age: 1 to 2

3 cups skim milk (for preparing
    pudding)
4-ounce package regular vanilla
    instant pudding mix
$1/2$ cup orange juice
Wooden craft sticks or plastic
    spoons
Molds or small paper cups

Mix milk and pudding, following package directions. Add orange juice. Insert wooden craft sticks
or plastic spoons before freezing. Freeze in molds
or small paper cups.

Variations:
Fudgesicles: Replace vanilla pudding mix with
    chocolate, and increase milk by $1/2$ cup.
Bananasicles: Replace vanilla pudding mix with
    banana, and increase milk by $1/2$ cup.

Shaggy Dogs

Age: 2 to 3

1 small (3-ounce) milk chocolate
    bar
1 tablespoon milk
1 bag large marshmallows
Sticks for toasting marshmallows
2 cups shredded, sweetened
    coconut

Unwrap chocolate bar, place in pan, add milk,
warm over low heat until it melts to make syrup.
Toast marshmallows on sticks, dip in syrup, and
then roll in coconut.

Theme Party for Independence Day Band Party

Age: 2 to 3

Toddlers can experience the freedom of Independence Day through a theme party.

Decorate in red, white, and blue, and play marching-band tapes. Create your own toddler band: You'll need paper plates taped together with macaroni inside for tambourines and empty oatmeal containers with lids for drums. Wrap ends of toilet-paper rolls with wax paper and rubber bands for kazoos. Kids can also make newspaper hats (or purchase white painters' caps or baseball caps that they can decorate with paint, glue, feathers, plastic stars, sparkles, and so on). Just be careful that decorating is carefully supervised, and beware of using items that look edible but aren't (such as uncooked beans or noodles or beads) or that are choking hazards for younger siblings.

Festive Ideas for the Fall Season

Fall is a great time of year. The leaves are changing colors, and children can still play outdoors. One of the most popular celebrations, Halloween, comes during this time of the year. You can start off the season by making foods from the harvest with your children. Here are a few recipes for a perfect fall afternoon.

Basic Apple Cider

Age: 1 to 3

2 quarts apple cider or apple
   juice
1 cinnamon stick
6 whole cloves
1 teaspoon allspice
¼ cup brown sugar

Simmer all ingredients 5 to 10 minutes in sauce-pan. Strain into mugs before serving.

Tip: Even though fresh apple cider from the farm stand may be tempting, always use pasteurized cider or juice to avoid possible food-borne illness.

Pumpkin Spook Seeds

Halloween is not complete without a pumpkin carving. Go to the local pumpkin patch if you have any in the area, to pick out that special pumpkin. After you've transformed your pumpkin into your very own jack-o'-lantern, roast the seeds for a special treat.

Age: 3

Pumpkin seeds
Cooking spray (with butter or
   olive oil base)
Salt

Preheat oven to 300 degrees Fahrenheit. Wash pumpkin seeds in a colander. Spread on paper towels to dry. Distribute the pumpkin seeds evenly on a cookie sheet and spray with cooking spray. Toss to coat evenly. Sprinkle seeds with salt, and roast 20 to 30 minutes, or until golden brown.

Activities and Games

Halloween is a great holiday for afternoon party games. Here are some ideas.

Spooks 'n' Goblins Party

You can take any of the ideas on the previous page and create a spooks 'n' goblins party by using these decoration ideas.

Use homemade jack-'o-lanterns for perfect centerpieces.

Place orange and black balloons under the table to add color and excitement to any party.

Decorate with pumpkin place cards to add to Halloween festivities. Purchase small pumpkins and write each guest's name on one.

Black Cat Cupcakes

Age: 3

Prepare any cake mix according to package directions. Pour into a paper-lined cupcake pan, and bake according to directions. Prepare basic frosting mix as directed on page 202. Frost cupcakes. Decorate each with a gumdrop cat: Slice 1-inch black gumdrops horizontally into three slices. Use small, rounded slice for head, largest slice for body; cut tail and ears from third slice.

Basic Frosting

2 egg whites
1½ cups sugar
¼ teaspoon cream of tartar
⅓ cup water
1 teaspoon vanilla
Red and yellow food coloring

Combine egg whites, sugar, cream of tartar, and water in top of double boiler. Beat 1 minute on high speed with electric mixer. Place over boiling water (water should not touch bottom of pan that contains egg white mixture); beat 7 minutes on high speed. Remove pan from heat; add vanilla and 1 or 2 drops of each food coloring to tint orange. Beat 2 minutes on high speed.

Fun Foods for the Winter Season

The most popular holidays fall in this wonderful time of the year. The days are shorter, and the weather is cooler—making it an ideal time to cuddle up with warm treats. Be careful of our sugar warnings at the beginning of this chapter.

Low-Sugar Cereal Mix

Age: 2 to 3

Cereals make great treats with nutritional value. Serve in colorful muffin pan liners. Wrap with plastic wrap and tie with a curly ribbon—instant party treats!

Mix together all of the cereal (1 cup each of four different low-sugar cereals). Add raisins and sunflower seeds. Mix. Store in tightly covered plastic containers.

4 cups low-sugar cereal (mixture of Cheerios, Total, Rice Chex, and Kix, for example)

1 cup raisins

1 cup toasted sunflower seeds

This time of year is especially good for getting creative with nutritious, colorful food. Here are some basic ideas:

Serve green vegetables in a tomato.

Make green pancakes, using green food coloring. Cut into the shape of a tree, and serve with red syrup (strawberry or raspberry). Add pomegranate seeds for light bulbs (only for children over four; younger children may choke on the seeds).

Form snowmen out of orange slices rolled in warm, sticky marshmallows (cut the oranges into different sizes).

Spread cookies with cream cheese frosting.

Here are some fun recipes to consider during the holidays.

Cream Cheese Frosting

Age: 1 to 2

3 ounces full-fat cream cheese

6 tablespoons unsalted butter, melted

1 teaspoon vanilla extract

2 cups powdered sugar

1 tablespoon milk

Bring cream cheese and butter to room temperature. Add vanilla and mix well. Gradually stir in powdered sugar and milk. Chill.

Sugar Cookies

Age: 1 to 2

8 tablespoons (1 stick) butter, softened

8 tablespoons (1 stick) margarine

1 cup sugar

1 egg

1 teaspoon vanilla extract

3 cups all-purpose flour

1 teaspoon baking powder

1/8 teaspoon salt

Preheat oven to 350 degrees Fahrenheit. Combine butter, margarine, and sugar in mixing bowl. Beat until fluffy, at least 5 minutes. Add egg and vanilla; beat. In separate bowl, mix together flour, baking powder, and salt. Sift into butter mixture. Beat well. Roll out or drop by spoonfuls onto baking sheet. Bake 10 minutes. Cool on cooling rack.

Candy Cane Cookies

Age: 1 to 2

Preheat oven to 350 degrees Fahrenheit. Prepare a recipe for sugar cookie dough (previous page), or use rolled cookie dough from the grocery store. Divide dough into three sections. Tint two sections different colors by working in a few drops of food coloring (try red and green). Divide the three sections into 1-inch balls. Roll each ball into a foot-long log. Lay out three logs of different colors parallel to each other, and twist from one end to the other. Shape in the form of candy canes. Bake 10 minutes. Cool on cooling rack.

Sugar cookie dough (previous recipe or store-bought)
Food coloring (red and green)

Gingerbread Trees

Age: 2 to 3

¼ cup unsalted butter

½ cup brown sugar

½ cup molasses

3½ cups unbleached all-
  purpose flour

1 teaspoon baking soda

⅛ teaspoon nutmeg

⅛ teaspoon ground cloves

½ teaspoon cinnamon

1 teaspoon powdered ginger

½ teaspoon salt

¼ cup water

Raisins

Preheat oven to 350 degrees Fahrenheit. Cream butter and brown sugar together in large bowl. Add molasses, and beat until well mixed. Sift together flour, baking soda, nutmeg, cloves, cinnamon, ginger, and salt in separate bowl. Add flour mixture and water to butter mixture. Beat thoroughly with strong spoon. Roll out dough on floured surface. Cut into shapes of trees or gingerbread people with a cutter. Put cookies on greased baking sheet. Decorate with raisins. Bake 7 to 9 minutes. Remove cookies; cool on rack.

Cherries Jubilee

Age: 1 to 2

Pour milk and ¼ teaspoon of the almond extract into large bowl. Add pudding mix. Beat 2 minutes with wire whisk. Stir in whipped topping. Mix pie filling and remaining extract. Spoon pudding mixture and pie filling alternately into dessert glasses. Refrigerate until ready to serve.

1¼ cups cold skim milk

½ teaspoon almond extract

1 package (4-serving size) instant Jell-O vanilla pudding and pie

1 cup thawed non-dairy "lite" whipped topping

20-ounce can "lite" cherry pie filling

Theme Party Ideas for the Winter Holidays

The winter season is good for gathering and letting children socialize with one another.

Cookie Exchange Party
Age: 2 to 3

This theme is based on sharing baked cookies throughout the holidays. Children get excited about making—and most of all sharing—fun, baked creations!

Two to three weeks before your party, send out invitations in the shape of a cookie to each child/parent on your guest list. Your invitation should explain that you are hosting a "cookie exchange" and that guests need to bring a dozen of their favorite

Stocking Stuffers

Here are some great ideas for stocking stuffers.

- Fill the stocking with recipes from a children's cookbook or with a shiny new kitchen tool, such as a wire whisk, tied with a festive ribbon.
- Put homemade candy such as peanut brittle in small plastic bags, and wrap in a colorful paper.
- Combine beautiful tangerines, shiny apples, and small packages of your favorite Christmas cookies.

holiday cookies and enough copies of the recipe for all to share. (If this is a kids' party, be sure to let your young guests know that Mom or Dad will need to help in preparing the cookies.)

For the party, prepare a presentation table on which to display everyone's gourmet holiday sweets. Provide each guest with a special cookie treat box. Each guest should select one cookie from each tray to place in their box to take home. Be sure to distribute the cookie recipes as well.

Other Special Holidays to Celebrate

There are many holidays around the world that are meaningful to celebrate. To help broaden your child's horizons, occasionally pick another culture's holiday, learn about it with your child, and adapt some of the food ideas in this chapter to celebrate it. Or try new foods from those cultures to broaden taste buds as well. Listed below are a few holidays your family might like to find out more about.

Kwanzaa

Kwanzaa is celebrated from December 26 to January 1, with each day focusing on one of the seven fundamental principles collectively known as the Nguzo Saba. Unlike most other holidays, Kwanzaa is not a religious, patriotic, or political celebration, but rather a cultural celebration that pays tribute to the strength of history, heritage, and spirit of the African-American people.

Hanukkah

Hanukkah is an eight-day Jewish holiday commemorating the rededication of the Temple of Jerusalem after its desecration by the tyrannical King Antiochus of Syria. Hanukkah occurs in late December; the dates vary each year.

The leaders of Israel declared that every year Jews should celebrate the miracle of Hanukkah, which means "dedication." They decided to kindle lights, one for each night, in commemoration of the miracle in the temple—the holiday is also known as the "Festival of Lights."

Chinese New Year

Whenever Chinese New Year is mentioned, the first thing that comes to the minds of most people is "What year is this?" This refers to the animal representation for that year. The designation is usually explained with a simple story that a long time ago, Buddha called together all the animals to help guard and protect the year. Of all the animals, only twelve answered the call. To establish an orderly sequence of months, a race was called. In the race, the Ox would have taken first place had it not been for the clever and cunning Rat, who rode on the back of the Ox and jumped forward at the finish line to steal the top award. Here, the order of the months is the order in which the animals finished the race.

CHAPTER 12

Recipes for Homemade Craft and Baby Supplies

To affect the quality of the day, that is the highest of arts.
—Henry David Thoreau

N ot all recipes are for food! Rather than purchase products such as play dough and finger paint, baby wipes and oils, you can save money by making your own. Here is a collection of tested recipes for practical inedibles for your child's use.

Crafts from Your Kitchen

If you spend a lot of time in your kitchen and you have children, life is easier for everyone if they can be in the kitchen with you—at least part of the time. In your child's world, *work* and *play* mean the same thing. So let's continue to have some fun with some basic "recipes" that come from the kitchen.

Basic Play Dough

Mix flour, salt, oil, and alum. Add desired amount of food coloring to ½ cup water. Gradually add colored water to dry ingredients until mixture is stiff like bread dough but not sticky. Add a little more water if necessary to get desired consistency. Store in airtight plastic container.

1 cup white flour

½ cup salt

2 tablespoons vegetable oil

1 teaspoon alum (a sticking compound found in most drug stores)

Food coloring

½ cup water

Molding Clay

This is a great way to make holiday decorations for hanging on walls or trees. Use indoors only, and store in resealable plastic bags to keep from year to year. If finished items get moist, they fall apart, so keep them dry.

Mix salt, water, and oil. Add flour. Make clay into different shapes. Bake 2 hours at 250 degrees Fahrenheit. Clay will harden. Paint as desired with purchased model paint.

1 cup salt

½ cup water

2 teaspoons vegetable oil

2 cups flour

Basic Finger Paint

Finger paints are fun for children. Keep a roll of white butcher paper handy (purchase at the craft or party store, or even the office supply store), and you'll always be prepared for a painting event. You won't want the paint on your walls or carpets, so set up a special place for painting. Perhaps the kitchen table if you have a linoleum floor, or an outdoor picnic table covered with plastic. Make it a place where you don't have to constantly remind them to be careful so they can concentrate on having fun and being creative!

3 teaspoons sugar

½ cup cornstarch

2 cups water

Food coloring

Pinch of detergent (keeps color
  from staining)

Baby food jars

Mix sugar and cornstarch. Add 2 cups water. Cook over low heat 8 minutes or until blended. Divide mixture into sections. Add a different food color (as much as desired) and a pinch of detergent to each section. Mix well with a metal spoon. Store each color in a baby food jar.

Clove Paste

Pastes like this one work well for working with sticky stuff like papier-mâché.

1 cup flour

1 cup sugar

1 teaspoon alum

4 cups water

0.5-ounce bottle of clove oil
  (sold in natural food stores)

In saucepan mix flour, sugar, alum, and water over medium heat for 5 minutes. Cook until clear and thick. Add drops of clove oil until desired smell is apparent. Cool. Store in covered container in refrigerator.

Keepsake Coasters

Create finger paint. Use scissors to cut a variety of colored paper into small squares and other shapes. Coat inside of plastic lid lightly with glue. Arrange construction paper in designs on glue, making a stained glass or mosaic effect. Let dry before using as a coaster.

Option: Use just one color of construction paper then paint with finger paint.

8- × 11-inch construction paper in a variety of colors
Plastic lids from yogurt or margarine containers
Glue
Finger paint (from earlier recipe)

Homemade Baby Supplies

Like homemade craft supplies, homemade baby care supplies can be more economical than store-bought ones. In addition, you can use more natural ingredients than what are found in the commercial varieties.

Basic Baby Wipes

Mix oils, and shake together with 1½ to 2 cups water in tightly closed, tall (larger than paper towel) plastic container. Gently mix in shampoo. Pour over a half-length roll of paper towels with the cardboard tube removed. Put lengthwise in container and dispense by pulling wipe from the inside of the roll.

⅛ cup mineral or baby oil
8 drops lavender essential oil (if wanted for scent)
5 drops tea tree essential oil
1½ to 2 cups water
1 to 2 tablespoons baby shampoo
Paper towels, last half of a roll

Antibacterial Baby Wipes

½ cup distilled water

¼ cup vinegar

¼ cup aloe vera gel

1 tablespoon calendula essential oil (sold at drug or natural food stores)

1 drop lavender essential oil

1 drop tea tree essential oil

Glass jar with a tight-fitting lid

Sturdy paper towels

Pour all liquid ingredients into jar, cover, and shake to blend. Place paper towels in separate container, and pour on enough solution to moisten. Roll towels into jar. (You can also use washcloths or flannel cloths for wipes.)

Note: If your baby has a really red, raw diaper rash, you'll want to avoid using these wipes because the vinegar and essential oils in them may cause a burning sensation.

Calendula Baby Oil

8 ounces of oil (olive, almond, apricot, or sunflower)

1 ounce calendula flowers (entire blossom)

Place the oil and flowers in a Crock-Pot on low temperature for about 4 hours to extract the beneficial properties of the calendula into the oil. Allow oil to cool, and then strain with cheesecloth or gauze. You can add a few drops of fragrant essential oils if you like. Try 5 to 10 drops each of orange and lavender or chamomile. Calendula offers a healing effect and may help prevent an overgrowth of yeast in the diaper area.

Celestial Baby Massage Oil

Pour your ingredients right into the bottle from which you will dispense the massage oil. Just give a good shake to blend the oils, and you're all set. Start out with the smaller amounts first, as some oils are very potent. If you want a truly heavenly oil, use rose essential oil in place of lavender and orange. You will like this so much that you may want to use it on yourself!

4 ounces of oil (olive, almond, apricot, or sunflower)

3 to 5 drops lavender essential oil

3 to 5 drops orange essential oil

Teething Gel

Add 1 drop clove oil to glycerin and shake until well blended. Taste to make sure it is not too strong before adding another drop. For a young baby, I use two drops. You can use vegetable oil instead of glycerin if you want. Glycerin is very sweet, so it makes the remedy a bit more appealing; glycerin also adheres to the gums a little better than vegetable oil.

2 drops essential oil of clove

1 ounce pure vegetable glycerin (sold at natural-food stores)

Baby Powder

Commercial baby powder contains talc, an ingredient that some people are concerned may cause lung problems when its dust is inhaled. Instead of putting your baby at possible risk, you can simply use cornstarch as a natural substitute for baby powder.

Cornstarch

Save a large spice jar that has a plastic shaker top—such as the kind you buy seasoned salt or meat tenderizer in. Wash and dry jar thoroughly. Fill with cornstarch. Replace the plastic shaker lid and use for all diaper changes.

BREASTFEEDING IN WORKPLACES AROUND THE WORLD

As discussed in the main text of the book, breastfeeding offers many advantages to both mother and child. Yet in the United States, only 54 percent of new mothers breastfeed when they leave the hospital to take their newborn home, while in Australia and Scandinavia, virtually all mothers continue breastfeeding when they are discharged from the hospital. For U.S. mothers who return to work, breastfeeding their child can be a challenge, even though it's valuable to the infant's health. This information is an interesting resource as you look at worldwide breastfeeding practices in the workplace.

Resource: Web site of Representative Carolyn Maloney, Fourteenth District, New York (http://www.house.gov/maloney /issues/breastfeeding)

International Labour Organization Breastfeeding Policy

The International Labour Organization (ILO) has created labor standards in all work-related matters (abolishing forced labor and allowing freedom of association, equality of opportunity, social security, maternity protection, child-labor laws, etc.). In 1919, the ILO concluded that a woman should be allowed to nurse her child two times a day for a period of one-half hour during the workday. In 1952, the ILO expanded maternity benefits by making paid nursing breaks available during working hours. More than three-fourths of the countries in the world conform to the following ILO standards of adequate maternity leave and time to breastfeed or express milk during the day:

- twelve weeks' maternity leave, with extension if necessary
- cash benefits during leave of at least 66 percent of previous earnings
- breastfeeding breaks totaling at least one hour per day
- prohibition of dismissal during maternity leave

Breastfeeding Policy in the United States

Unfortunately, most companies in the United States do not provide routine nursing breaks for mothers in the workplace. This makes it difficult for working mothers to follow the American Academy of Pediatrics' recommendation to breastfeed for at least the first twelve months of a child's life. You are therefore encouraged to urge companies in your area to follow many other nations' examples and allow breastfeeding breaks so new mothers can either nurse their children or express milk so that nursing can continue.

Breastfeeding Policy in Other Countries

The following paragraphs briefly discuss how various countries support breastfeeding in the workplace.

Egypt

For eighteen months after delivery, women are granted two daily breaks of not less than half an hour each. Breaks may be combined if the female employee so desires. These breaks are in addition to the normal breaks granted to employees generally and do not result in any reduction of pay.

Tunisia

For nine months after delivery, a woman employee has two paid half-hour breaks to breastfeed, in addition to the normal break times. Employers are required to provide breastfeeding rooms for their employees.

Argentina

Working mothers of nursing babies have the right to two daily half-hour breaks for breastfeeding during work time for one year after the baby is born.

Canada

In British Columbia, employers are required to accommodate women who wish to breastfeed children during work hours unless their absence would cause undue hardship.

France

Nursing mothers are allowed to take two one-hour breaks from work. The employer must provide nursing rooms—or breastfeeding rooms, as they're sometimes called.

Israel

For four months after delivery, a nursing mother may be absent from work one hour a day, as long as she is employed in a full-time job. The employee's pay will not be deducted for the absence.

People's Republic of China

The law provides for two thirty-minute breaks each working shift for the nursing of infants up to age one and the establishment of health clinics, breastfeeding rooms, and child-care centers.

Italy

Full-time working women are allowed two paid one-hour breaks to breastfeed. A woman who works six hours is entitled to a one-hour break for breastfeeding, which can be split into two half-hour breaks.

Japan

A full-time employee who is nursing is granted two thirty-minute breaks a day in addition to set break periods. Part-time employees who are nursing are allowed one thirty-minute break. The breaks are paid if there is a collective agreement in the workplace to pay for the breaks.

Norway

Working women are allowed two hours daily to breastfeed at work, and 99 percent of mothers are still breastfeeding after six weeks.

Russia

Nursing mothers are granted thirty-minute breaks at least every three hours. Breaks for a nursing child are included in work time and are paid according to the nursing mother's average earnings.

Turkey

Breastfeeding mothers are allowed two forty-five-minute periods to nurse. These periods are considered work hours.

Mozambique

Two half-hour paid nursing breaks are provided during the workday for up to six months.

Sweden

A woman can take breaks to breastfeed her child as she wishes.

WEB SITES FOR BUSY PARENTS

Listed below are a number of Web sites that provide information on pregnancy, breastfeeding, and parenting in general; some of them have sections for your children to enjoy, too.

Parenting

Welcome to Parent Soup!

www.parentsoup.com

Welcome to your very own oasis of information and community called Parent Soup. While here, you can:

Visit the bulletin boards, where parents exchange advice and information and where experts answer your questions.

Chat live with other Parent Soupers.

Check out the many departments.

Search a vast array of parenting resources.

Here at Parent Soup, from the comfort of your own home, at whatever time of day or night, you can check in to ask a question, connect with other concerned and involved parents, ask an expert, and have a little fun. The real advantage of the Parent

Soup community is that it's always there—ready to hear you sigh, take your question, boost you back up, or just listen. And that's no small thing when you're a parent.

Parents Place

www.parentsplace.com

This site provides information about the pregnancy and new babies to great parenting advice. You'll find an "ask experts" section, live chats, and tools such as an interactive birth planner and a pregnancy calendar.

Family.com

www.family.com

A world of information and inspiration for raising young children.

KidSource OnLine

www.kidsource.com

The source for education, health care, and product information that will make a difference in the lives of parents and their children.

The CyberMom Dot Com

www.thecybermom.com

A resource for mothers on the Web.

Pregnancy/Newborns

Childbirth.org

www.childbirth.org

Childbirth.org: The Ultimate Pregnancy and Birth Site. Pregnancy is a very special time in a woman's life. Educating yourself to be a good consumer, knowing your options, and how to provide yourself with the best possible care is essential to a healthy pregnancy. Enjoy the many links of educational, informational, and personal nature.

Storknet

www.storknet.org

Storknet—The Pregnancy and Parent Online Community is a resource for parents-to-be and new parents. It includes a weekly calendar of what to expect during pregnancy.

PillowTalk's Stork Site

www.storksite.com

Your complete pregnancy and childbirth resource center! Walk through your pregnancy comfortably and sensibly. If you are pregnant, are a supporting partner, or simply want to learn all you can about these wonderful and mysterious nine months, you'll find it all here.

Breastfeeding

Congresswoman Carolyn Maloney Reports

www.breastfeeding.org/maloney.htm

Congresswoman Maloney's Web site contains the latest information on breastfeeding legislation, as discussed in previous appendices.

La Leche League International

www.lalecheleague.org

This Web site is sponsored by La Leche League International, an international, nonprofit, nonsectarian organization dedicated to providing education, information, support, and encouragement to women who want to breastfeed. All breastfeeding mothers, as well as future breastfeeding mothers, are welcome to come to their free meetings or call their leaders for breastfeeding help. They also provide healthcare professionals with continuing-education opportunities and the latest research on lactation management.

Medical Resources

Dr. Greene's HouseCalls

www.drgreene.com

The goal of this site is to equip women with pediatric information. So please, send your questions, and watch your children grow! *Notice:* All pages and their content are provided as information only. This is not a substitute for medical care or your doctor's attention. Please seek the advice of your pediatrician or family doctor. This site presents data as is, without any warranty of any kind, express or implied. It is impossible to cover every eventuality in any answer, which makes direct contact with your health-care provider imperative.

Child Nutrition

American Academy of Pediatrics

www.aap.org

This site contains information for professional education, advocacy, research, publications, and consumers.

Children's Nutrition Research Center

www.bcm.tmc.edu

One of six USDA/ARS human nutrition research centers, this is dedicated to defining the nutrient needs of healthy children, from conception through adolescence, and pregnant and nursing women.

Dietary Guidelines for Healthy Children

www.americanheart.org

The American Heart Association provides information and links to sites about infants and diet, obesity in children, high blood pressure in children, and related topics.

Family Food Zone

www.familyfoodzone.com

A "cyberfridge" full of advice on kids cooking, Mom's food pyramid, shopping tips, and references.

The Baby Gourmet

www.TheBabyGourmet.com (not available until mid-2001)

A virtual wonderland of baby recipes, wholesome snacks, and fun ideas.

Fresh Starts

www.freshstarts.com

This offers resources that can help you maintain proper nutrition, including lesson plans for teachers, exciting activities for students, and tasty recipes for parents.

NNCC Nutrition Database

www.nncc.org

The National Network for Child Care nutrition database offers articles on child nutrition, infants, breastfeeding, snacks, and food safety.

No Bones About It!

www.drink-milk.com

This interactive site for nine-to-fourteen-year-olds, parents, and teachers contains calcium-packed snack recipes, a food personality quiz, and much more. Teachers can download lesson plans for classroom use.

KidsHealth—Children's Health and Parenting Info

www.kidshealth.org

The articles on this site cover issues of nutrition and exercise and how they affect children's health.

PedInfo

www.pedinfo.org

This is an index of the pediatric Internet from the University of Alabama at Birmingham, which is dedicated to the dissemination of online information for pediatricians and others interested in child health.

USDA Food and Nutrition Service

www.fns.usda.gov

This site contains information about the nutrition services offered by the U.S. Department of Agriculture. The USDA provides children and needy families better access to a more healthful diet. In this site you will find news releases, speeches, and food-safety information, as well as all the latest communications to Congress involving food.

Health in News

www.HealthInNews.com

This site offers current news on health-related topics by medical experts, as well as literature on the latest topics such as nutrition, baby care, and parenting.

WEIGHTS AND MEASURES

Approximate Metric Equivalents (Dry Ingredients by Weight)

One ounce contains approximately 28 grams. If you need to convert ounces to grams, you can do so easily, and approximately, by multiplying the number of ounces by 30. To convert grams to ounces, simply divide by 30.

1 ounce   = $\frac{1}{16}$ pound   = 30 grams
4 ounces   = $\frac{1}{4}$ pound   = 120 grams
8 ounces   = $\frac{1}{2}$ pound   = 240 grams
12 ounces   = $\frac{3}{4}$ pound   = 360 grams
16 ounces   = 1 pound   = 480 grams

Cooking/Oven Temperatures

	Fahrenheit	Celsius
Freeze water	32 degrees	0 degrees
Room temperature	68 degrees	20 degrees
Boil water	212 degrees	100 degrees
Bake	325 degrees	160 degrees

Fahrenheit	Celsius
350	180
375	190
400	200
425	220
450	230

Approximate Conversion to Metric Measures

¼ teaspoon = 1 milliliter

½ teaspoon = 2 milliliters

1 teaspoon = 5 milliliters

3 teaspoons = 1 tablespoon = ½ fluid ounce = 15 milliliters

2 tablespoons = ⅛ cup = 1 fluid ounce = 30 milliliters

4 tablespoons = ¼ cup = 2 fluid ounces = 60 milliliters

5⅓ tablespoons = ⅓ cup = 3 fluid ounces = 80 milliliters

8 tablespoons = ½ cup = 4 fluid ounces = 120 milliliters

10⅔ tablespoons = ⅔ cup = 5 fluid ounces = 160 milliliters

12 tablespoons = ¾ cup = 6 fluid ounces = 180 milliliters

16 tablespoons = 1 cup = 8 fluid ounces = 250 milliliters

1 pint = 2 cups = 16 fluid ounces = 480 milliliters

2 pints = 4 cups = 32 fluid ounces = 960 milliliters

1 quart = 4 cups = 32 fluid ounces = 960 milliliters

33 fluid ounces = 1,000 milliliters (1 liter)

4 quarts = 1 gallon

INDEX

Rice (*continued*)
  pudding, riza galo, 155
  spanakoryzo, 154
  vegetable soup, 158
Riza Galo, 155

S

Sandwiches
  banana, 177
  bunny, 194
  tuna, sleep tight, 174
Savory lentils, 153
Selenium, 35–36
Shaggy dogs, 198
Shaw, George Bernard, 1
SIDS. *see* Sudden infant death
    syndrome
Sippy cups, 60, 61
Sleep, restful, 173
Sleep tight tuna sandwiches, 174
Sodium, 32–33
Solid foods
  best, 84–85
  bonding and, 12–13
  commercial
    costs, 10
    homemade *vs.*, 10–12
    labels, 5–6
    marketing, 3
    nutrients, 4
    right, choosing, 3
    safety tips, 54
    taste, 12
  homemade
    commercial *vs.*, 10–12
    freezing, 77–80
    nutrients, 4
    preparation
      blending purees, 76–77
      cleanliness, 66–67

contamination, 65–66
cooking methods, 71–74
cooling, 74, 76
equipment, 68–70
general tips, 75
methods, 67–68
refrigeration, 67
sterilizing, 68
taste, 12
thawing, 80–81
warming, 81–82
intermediate, about, 120–123
introducing
  age-specific list, 26–28
  cereals, 53–56
  developmental factors, 49–
      52
  fruits, 58–59
  meats, 59–60
  vegetables, 57–58
serving size, 7
switching to, 83
for toddlers, about, 130–132
Soups
  barley broth, 172
  carrot-bean, 126
  cheese and vegetable, 151
  chicken, tomorrow, 146
  de Christophe, 150
  egg drop with rice, 161
  fish, Poseidon's, 156
  golden carrot-rice, 125
  lentil, thick, 92
  mint, hint of, 124
  peanut butter, 125
  split pea, 92
  split pea and ham, 124
  vegetable
    creamy, 123
    Grandma Parsons', 144

International Conversion Chart

These are not exact equivalents; they have been slightly rounded to make measuring easier.

Liquid Measurements

American	Imperial	Metric	Australian
2 tablespoons (1 oz.)	1 fl. oz.	30 ml	1 tablespoon
¼ cup (2 oz.)	2 fl. oz.	60 ml	2 tablespoons
⅓ cup (3 oz.)	3 fl. oz.	80 ml	¼ cup
½ cup (4 oz.)	4 fl. oz.	125 ml	⅓ cup
⅔ cup (5 oz.)	5 fl. oz.	165 ml	½ cup
¾ cup (6 oz.)	6 fl. oz.	185 ml	⅔ cup
1 cup (8 oz.)	8 fl. oz.	250 ml	¾ cup

Spoon Measurements

American	Metric
¼ teaspoon	1 ml
½ teaspoon	2 ml
1 teaspoon	5 ml
1 tablespoon	15 ml

Weights

US/UK	Metric
1 oz.	30 grams (g)
2 oz.	60 g
4 oz. (¼ lb)	125 g
5 oz. (⅓ lb)	155 g
6 oz.	185 g
7 oz.	220 g
8 oz. (½ lb)	250 g
10 oz.	315 g
12 oz. (¾ lb)	375 g
14 oz.	440 g
16 oz. (1 lb)	500 g
2 lbs	1 kg

Oven Temperatures

Farenheit	Centigrade	Gas
250	120	½
300	150	2
325	160	3
350	180	4
375	190	5
400	200	6
450	230	8

Honour

ELIF SHAFAK

PENGUIN BOOKS

PENGUIN BOOKS

Published by the Penguin Group

Penguin Books Ltd, 80 Strand, London WC2R ORL, England

Penguin Group (USA) Inc., 375 Hudson Street, New York, New York 10014, USA

Penguin Group (Canada), 90 Eglinton Avenue East, Suite 700, Toronto, Ontario, Canada M4P 2Y3
(a division of Pearson Penguin Canada Inc.)

Penguin Ireland, 25 St Stephen's Green, Dublin 2, Ireland (a division of Penguin Books Ltd)

Penguin Group (Australia), 707 Collins Street, Melbourne, Victoria 3008, Australia
(a division of Pearson Australia Group Pty Ltd)

Penguin Books India Pvt Ltd, 11 Community Centre, Panchsheel Park, New Delhi – 110 017, India

Penguin Group (NZ), 67 Apollo Drive, Rosedale, Auckland 0632, New Zealand
(a division of Pearson New Zealand Ltd)

Penguin Books (South Africa) (Pty) Ltd, Block D, Rosebank Office Park,
181 Jan Smuts Avenue, Parktown North, Gauteng 2193, South Africa

Penguin Books Ltd, Registered Offices: 80 Strand, London WC2R ORL, England

www.penguin.com

First published by Viking 2012
Published in Penguin Books 2013
004

Typeset by Jouve (UK), Milton Keynes
Printed in Great Britain by Clays Ltd, St Ives plc

ISBN: 978–0–670–92116–4

www.greenpenguin.co.uk